TRANSACTIONS OF THE
AMERICAN PHILOSOPHICAL SOCIETY
HELD AT PHILADELPHIA
FOR PROMOTING USEFUL KNOWLEDGE

VOLUME 68, PART 7 · 1978

France and the Arab Middle East 1914–1920

JAN KARL TANENBAUM
ASSOCIATE PROFESSOR OF HISTORY, FLORIDA STATE UNIVERSITY

THE AMERICAN PHILOSOPHICAL SOCIETY

INDEPENDENCE SQUARE: PHILADELPHIA

October 1978

For
Joanne, Michelle, Stephanie, Nadine

Copyright © 1978 by The American Philosophical Society
Library of Congress Catalog
Card Number 78–068379
International Standard Book Number 0–87169–687–8
US ISSN 0065–9746

PREFACE

The purpose of this study is to delineate France's Middle Eastern policies during World War I and the ensuing peace conference. In so doing, the study will show how France was able to gain control of Syria and Lebanon in 1920.

In 1914 France held a dominant financial and cultural position in the Arab Middle East. During the next six years of war and peace, France's long-standing position in the Middle East was greatly jeopardized. Great Britain, which dominated the Allies' wartime Middle Eastern military effort against Turkey and monopolized the Allies' wartime diplomatic relations with the Arabs, resented the French presence in the area. The Arabs, encouraged by Great Britain and the Wilsonian ideals of self-determination, also opposed French colonialism. Yet it was France, not England and the Arabs, which determined the postwar political settlement in Syria and Lebanon. In 1920 French troops landed in Syria, thereby assuring that France would have effective control of both Lebanon and Syria for the next two decades.

In the course of this study I have benefited from the assistance of several institutions: in France, the Archives du Ministère des Affaires Etrangères, Bibliothèque de l'Institut de France, Archives Centrales de la Marine, Archives du Ministère de la Guerre (Service Historique and Section Outre-Mer); and in England, the Public Record Office, the House of Lords Record Office, and the India Office and Records.

I also wish to thank the Florida State University for a Faculty Development Grant which allowed me a respite from my teaching duties. Finally, I owe an immense debt of gratitude to my parents and family for their support and encouragement over many years. This work is dedicated to my wife and daughters, Joanne, Michelle, Stephanie, and Nadine.

J.K.T.

ABBREVIATIONS

AAE	Archives du Ministère des Affaires Etrangères, Quai d'Orsay, Paris
AMG	Archives du Ministère de la Guerre, Château de Vincennes, Vincennes
Archives Marine	Archives Centrales de la Marine, Château de Vincennes, Vincennes
BD	*Documents on British Foreign Policy, 1919–1939*
Cab.	Cabinet Office Papers, Public Record Office, London
F.O.	Foreign Office Papers, Public Record Office, London
Levant S-L-C	Série: Levant, 1918–1929, Syrie-Liban-Cilicie at the AAE.
USFR	*Papers Relating to the Foreign Relations of the United States, 1919: The Paris Peace Conference*

FRANCE AND THE ARAB MIDDLE EAST, 1914–1920

Jan Karl Tanenbaum

CONTENTS

	PAGE
1. France and the wartime agreements	5
2. The Arabs, British, and Zionists, 1916–1918	15
3. French failure in Paris	26
4. Apparent success	32
5. Road to Damascus	37
6. Conclusion	42
Appendix	
1. The Anglo-French Agreement of 1916	43
2. The Provisional Agreement of January 6, 1920	44
Bibliography	45
Index	49

1. FRANCE AND THE WARTIME AGREEMENTS

In 1914 the Ottoman Empire ruled most of the Arab Middle East. However, since the Crusades of the eleventh and twelfth centuries, France had established extremely close cultural, economic, financial, and religious ties with Syria, Lebanon, and Palestine.[1] The Turks, upon conquering Constantinople in the fifteenth century, recognized France's preeminent position in the Levant. During the next few centuries the Ottoman Empire acknowledged that France had the right to protect all Christians in the Levant, agreed that French citizens could not be tried in Turkish courts, and granted French entrepreneurs the concessions to build railways in Syria and harbors and ports in Beirut, Tripoli, Jaffa, and Haifa.

France's long-favored position in the Levant was not seriously challenged until the eve of World War I. British colonial officials now wanted to annex Syria to Egypt. Italy's fast-expanding religious orders, attempting to take advantage of France's anticlerical domestic program, sought to oust France from her role as defender of the Catholics in the Middle East. The Baghdad Railway ominously increased Germany's role in Anatolia, to the north of Syria.[2] The threat to France's position had become so unsettling that Premier Raymond Poincaré announced to the French Senate on December 21, 1912, that

in Syria and Lebanon we have traditional interests and we intend to see that they are respected.... We ourselves are resolved to maintain the integrity of the Ottoman Empire, but we shall not abandon any of our traditions there, nor repudiate any of the sympathies we have acquired, nor leave any of our interests there in abeyance.[3]

Georges Leygues, chairman of the Chamber Foreign Affairs Committee, agreed that, if the decaying Ottoman Empire were to disintegrate, France expected to be the dominant power in Lebanon, Syria, and Palestine. In the spring of 1914 he decried the intensified Italian and German economic, cultural, and diplomatic penetration of the Middle East. Current French policy in the eastern Mediterranean, Leygues clearly announced, "is not an ambitious policy, but it cannot be and will never be a policy of renunciation."[4]

When Turkey entered World War I in 1914 on the side of Germany and Austria, Russia was more than willing to recognize France's sphere of interest in the Levant. Russia expected to receive something in return. In November, 1914, the czar told the French ambassador, Maurice Paléologue, that it was time to consider the postwar settlement. Russia wanted to control the Straits and to have Constantinople placed under international jurisdiction. Paléologue promptly took this opportunity to remind the czar that France "possesses a considerable patrimony of historical traditions and material interests in Syria, [Lebanon], and Palestine."[5]

Five months later, in March, 1915, the czar announced that Russia would annex the Straits and Constantinople. If France supported the czar's plan, the czar would support French claims in other regions of the Ottoman Empire.[6] Paléologue surprised the czar when he immediately demanded the terri-

---

[1] Before 1920 the term Syria had many meanings. In its most comprehensive sense it comprised modern Syria, Lebanon, Jordan, Israel, and the Turkish regions of Cilicia and Aintab, Urfa, and Marash. In its most restricted sense Syria referred to the Ottoman province of Damascus.

For the purposes of this study, the terms Lebanon and Syria refer to the approximate geographical boundaries of the present Lebanese and Syrian republics. The term Palestine refers to the approximate geographical boundaries of the present Israeli republic, including the west bank of the Jordan River.

[2] William I. Shorrock, *French Imperialism in the Middle East: The Failure of Policy in Syria and Lebanon, 1900–1914* (Madison, 1976).

[3] France, Assemblée Nationale, *Journal officiel, Sénat, Débats parlementaires,* Dec. 21, 1912, p. 340.

[4] Quoted in *Correspondance d'Orient,* no. 133 (Apr. 1, 1914): p. 296.

[5] Paléologue to Théophile Delcassé, French minister of foreign affairs, Nov. 22, 1914, Archives du Ministère des Affaires Etrangères, Quai d'Orsay, Paris (hereafter cited as AAE), série: A Paix, vol. 128. See also Paléologue to Delcassé, Sept. 26, 28, 1914, *ibid.*

[6] Paléologue to Delcassé, Mar. 4, 5, 1915, *ibid.*

tory stretching from the Taurus Mountains and Cilicia to the Sinai and from the Mediterranean to the Tigris River.[7] Paléologue believed that the ports of Alexandretta, Adana, and Mersina, together with a large portion of the Baghdad railway, would offer postwar economic opportunities for French industrialists and financiers.[8] Czar Nicholas II wondered how France would rule this vast terrain. Would it be annexed the way Algeria had been? Would it be a vast Arab kingdom under a French protectorate? The French had as yet no clear plans for the area. All that Paléologue wanted from Russia was recognition that France would have "all liberty of action in her new domain."[9]

By mid-March Nicholas II had accepted all of France's territorial demands except one: he refused to give France sole control of Palestine.[10] Denied Palestine, France initially did not accept Russia's annexationist plans. However, British diplomatic pressure and fears of increased German influence at Petrograd forced France on April 9 to notify the czar that she recognized Russia's claims to the Straits and Constantinople; in return, Russia was expected to support France's postwar Middle East territorial demands. Although the question of Palestine had been left dangling, all other French claims had been recognized.[11] Reviewing the intermittent Russo-French negotiations of the past six months, Paléologue cynically observed: "What could France do but yield to the Allies' claims and stipulate corresponding benefits for herself?"[12]

Although Russia had given France a free hand in a greatly enlarged Syria, French troops were still not there. When World War I broke out, some members of the French diplomatic corps recommended that France intervene militarily in the Levant. It was argued that failure to send French troops to Syria or Lebanon would give France's pre-war colonial competitors, above all England, an opportunity to move into the area. An Allied military campaign in Syria without large-scale French participation would be a "catastrophe." It could be a repetition of 1882 when French failure to partake in military action against Egypt resulted in England taking Egypt.[13]

German pressure on the Western Front, however, prevented France from undertaking a campaign in the Levant.[14] Blocked from Syria, France was determined to prevent England from going there. In December, 1914, when Winston Churchill, First Lord of the Admiralty, announced that the Dardanelles campaign would also include a British landing at Alexandretta, the French government protested.[15] The British understood the meaning of the French protest; a few weeks later the British Cabinet informed the French government that England had no intention of landing at Alexandretta.[16] Victor Augagneur, the French minister of the navy, promptly thanked Churchill for Britain's consideration. Augagneur also cautioned Churchill that any future military action against the Syrian coast could be initiated only "after an agreement, considering the undertaking as much from the military point of view as from the political point of view, was reached by the two governments."[17]

During much of 1915 French colonial societies, economic and political pressure groups, and colonial and military authorities urged that French troops be sent into the Levant in order to assure that France would control Syria when the postwar territorial settlements were determined. Many reasons were put forth to justify French claims to Cilicia, Syria, Lebanon, and Palestine. France had been the traditional protector of the Middle East Christians. France's future economic well-being depended upon trade with Cilicia, Beirut, and Damascus. The possession of Damascus, one of the most important Moslem cities, would increase France's prestige among her North African Moslem subjects. France had a civilizing mission to fulfill. France's prestige and honor were at stake. France had large-scale financial and industrial investments in the Middle East and these had to be secured. All of the reasons advanced to justify French imperialism were characterized by one basic concern: fear that Britain would move France out of the Middle East.[18]

---

[7] Paléologue to Delcassé, Mar. 17, 1915, *ibid*.

[8] Paléologue to Camille Barrère, French ambassador to Italy, Mar. 20, 1915, *ibid*., vol. 130.

[9] Paléologue to Delcassé, Mar. 17, 1915, *ibid*., vol. 128.

[10] *Ibid*.; Delcassé to Paléologue, Mar. 17, 1915, *ibid*.; Quai d'Orsay memo, "Syrie," Aug. 31, 1915, *ibid*.

[11] Delcassé to Paléologue, Apr. 9, 1915, *ibid*.; Paléologue to Delcassé, Apr. 13, 1915, *ibid*.

[12] Paléologue to Delcassé, Apr. 15, 1915, *ibid*.

[13] Jules-Albert Defrance, French ambassador to Egypt, to Delcassé, Nov. 9, 13, 1914, AAE, série: Guerre 1914–1918, vol. 867, fols. 30, 35. For similar views held by François Georges-Picot, serving in the French embassy in Cairo at this time, see Defrance to Delcassé, Nov. 5, Dec. 23, 1914, *ibid*., fols. 26, 110.

[14] Delcassé to Defrance, Nov. 13, 1914, *ibid*., fol. 33. A limited French landing on the Syrian coast was given some consideration. See Quai d'Orsay memo, "Considérations générales sur l'opportunité d'une intervention," Jan., 1915, *ibid*., fol. 149.

[15] Capitaine de Vaisseau Jean-Charles Le Gouz de Saint-Seine, French naval attaché at London, to Admiral Marie-Jacques-Charles Aubert, Jan. 18, 1915, *ibid*., vol. 1060, fol. 7; Saint-Seine to Victor Augagneur, French minister of the navy, Jan. 19, 1915, *ibid*., fol. 9.

[16] Churchill to Augagneur, Jan. 27, 1915, *ibid*., fol. 18.

[17] Augagneur to Churchill, Jan. 31, 1915, *ibid*., fol. 24. This letter is quoted in George H. Cassar, *The French and the Dardanelles: A Study of Failure in the Conduct of War* (London, 1971), p. 253.

[18] General Maurice-Camille Bailloud, "Note sur la ques-

Was there any foundation for French fears during the first year of the war? As early as November, 1914, Horatio Kitchener, British war minister, foresaw the possibility of using British-controlled Arabs to oust France from Syria:

> Supposing that the Arabs took up against the Turks, I think it would be our policy to recognize a new Khalif at Mecca or Medina . . . and guarantee the Holy Places from foreign aggression as well as from all internal interference. If this were done there appears to me to be a possibility for allowing Syria to be organized as an Arab state under the Khalif but also under European consular control and European guidance as regards Government.
>
> France would be greatly weakened by having Syria which is not a remunerative possession and which from its geographical position must lead France astray from her real objective: Tunis, Algeria, Morocco.
>
> I believe it is more sentiment than anything else which induces France to keep up her influence in Syria and if we frankly said, we do not want Syria, they would probably say the same and allow the formation of an Arab state that would enable the new Khalifate to have sufficient revenue to exist on.
>
> When there are signs of its realisation it will be time enough to recommend the matter to France and induce her to accept the situation.[19]

Several months later Sir Reginald Wingate, British governor-general of the Sudan, suggested a clearer notion of Kitchener's proposals. Although Wingate acknowledged that a portion of Syria would "presumably" go to France, his suggestions for the future of the Middle East emphasized England's role. It was not impossible that in the dim future a federation of semi-independent Arab states might exist under European guidance and supervision, linked together by racial and linguistic bonds, owing spiritual allegiance to a single Arab Primate, and looking to Great Britain as its Patron and Protector.[20]

Henry McMahon, British high commissioner to Egypt, proposed that England could gain control of Syria in a more subtle and less complicated fashion. Why worry about caliphs when England need only "concentrate [her] energies on Alexandretta with a view to the permanent occupation of that port. Possession of it would in course of time settle the Syrian problem of itself."[21] Ronald Storrs, British Oriental Secretary at the Residency in Cairo, emphasized that England must control Syria if Great Britain hoped to control the postwar Middle East:

> Syria is not only a goal per se but also a necessity both with regard to Irak and the Arabian peninsula. If, as would seem the ideal solution, we could make this latter into a sort of Afghanistan uncontrolled and independent within, but carrying on its foreign relations through us, we should be giving a maximum of satisfaction and assuming a minimum of responsibility; but the plan is not feasible unless we hold Syria.[22]

Sir Edward Grey, British foreign secretary, rejected all these suggestions because "it would mean a break with France if we put forward any claims in Syria and Lebanon."[23]

Although in early 1915 France was apprehensive that General John Maxwell's troops at the Suez Canal would move northward against the Turks and, in the process, spill into Syria,[24] the French government was greatly upset when it first learned of Britain's postwar proposals for the Middle East. On July 28, 1915, Sir Mark Sykes, Conservative member of Parliament sent by Kitchener to study the Middle East situation, informed French officials in Cairo that England would need a line of communications between India and the Mediterranean. In the postwar settlement England would take Mesopotamia including the cities of Baghdad and Mosul. From Mesopotamia, England would need a railway to the Mediterranean. The shortest route would be from Mesopotamia to Akaba and then westward to

---

tion syrienne," Jan. 1, 1915, Archives du Ministère de la Guerre, Service historique, Château de Vincennes, Vincennes (hereafter cited as AMG), 6N 33, dossier 8; document prepared for the Etat-Major Général, "Projet de débarquement d'un corps expéditionnaire en Orient," Jan. 20, 1915, AMG, 7N 2144, dossier: Opérations en Syrie; Admiral Pierre-Joseph Darrieus, interim commander of the French Eastern Mediterranean Fleet, to Augagneur, Sept. 22, 1915, ibid., dossier: Action navale; Defrance to Delcassé, Feb. 13, 1915, AAE, série: Guerre 1914–1918, vol. 868, fol. 34; Marseilles Chamber of Commerce to Delcassé, July, 1915, ibid., vol. 869, fol. 130; Comité de l'Asie française to Delcassé, Aug., 1915, ibid., vol. 870, fol. 73; Admiral Louis Dartige du Fournet, commander of the French Eastern Mediterranean Fleet, to Augagneur, July 21, 1915, ibid., fol. 3; report by Lieutenant René Doynel de Saint-Quentin, French military attaché with the British army in Egypt, "Visées anglaises sur la Syrie," to Alexandre Millerand, French war minister, July 28, 1915, Archives Centrales de la Marine, Château de Vincennes, Vincennes (hereafter cited as Archives Marine), carton Ea 199; Senator Etienne Flandin, "Nos Droits en Syrie et en Palestine," *La Revue hebdomadaire* **4** (1915): pp. 17–32; Charles Vincent, "La Syrie," *ibid.* **5** (1915): pp. 281–302.

[19] Kitchener to Edward Grey, British foreign secretary, Nov. 11, 1914, Papers of Sir Edward Grey, Foreign Office Papers, Public Record Office, London (hereafter cited as F.O.), 800/102. The letter is quoted in Elie Kedourie, *In the Anglo-Arab Labyrinth: The McMahon-Husayn Correspondence and Its Interpretations, 1914–1939* (Cambridge, 1976), p. 32.

[20] Wingate, "Note," Aug. 25, 1915, F.O. 371, vol. 2486, file 34982, paper 138500. Hereafter F.O. 371 references will be cited in this order: volume, file, paper.

[21] McMahon to Grey, Feb. 4, 1915, Grey Papers, F.O. 800/48.

[22] Storrs to his parents, Feb. 22, 1915, quoted in Kedourie, 1976: p. 33.

[23] Grey to McMahon, Mar. 8, 1915, Grey Papers, F.O. 800/48.

[24] Lieutenant Colonel Maucorps, head of the French military mission in Cairo, "Note sur une expédition en Syrie-Palestine," Feb. 2, 1915, AAE, série: Guerre 1914–1918, vol. 868, fol. 142; Millerand to Delcassé, Mar. 2, 1915, ibid., fol. 108; Millerand to Delcassé, July 10, 1915, ibid., vol. 869, fol. 100.

the Suez Canal. If this were possible, England would willingly allow France to have Syria and Palestine. Unfortunately, shifting desert sands made it impossible to build a railroad to the Suez Canal. England would thus have to build its railway from Mesopotamia to Haifa by way of Damascus. Sykes then elaborated. The Sherif of Mecca would take Damascus. France and England would take Tadmor in eastern Syria. England would have Palestine while Russia would control Jerusalem and the Holy Places. England would supply all of the advisers to the Turkish sultans, and France would be left with a protectorate over the Adana-Alexandretta region.[25] French reaction to Sykes's proposals was immediate. The government of René Viviani informed England that "Syria [and Palestine and Lebanon] along with Cilicia constitute a special zone for France and her interests would permit no partition there."[26] Ominously, French Foreign Minister Théophile Delcassé warned that British plans for Syria and Palestine "cannot continue without the risk of one day posing a problem to Anglo-French relations."[27]

In October, 1915, a series of events convinced the British that it was necessary to initiate discussions with the French in order to clarify their respective territorial aspirations in the Middle East. First, Kitchener was giving up on the ill-fated Dardanelles campaign and he expected to utilize Britain's Gallipoli troops in a Syrian campaign against the Turks. Second, Kitchener believed that the French Balkan campaign would fail in its basic mission to save Serbia and prevent the link up of the Bulgarian and Austro-German forces. The English incorrectly thought that the French would then pull out of the Balkans and send their troops to the Middle East against the Turks.[28] A third consideration was the British attempt to persuade Sherif Hussein of Mecca, the ruler of the Hejaz in western Arabia, to revolt against the Turks. If the revolt were forthcoming, the British in the summer of 1915 promised Hussein an independent Arabia. The Sherif, however, told Henry McMahon that he wanted more. He demanded British support for an independent Arab state. That state would stretch from Mersina on the Mediterranean eastward to the Persian border, then south to the Indian Ocean, and finally westward to the Red Sea.[29] The British Foreign Office was acutely aware that it could not consent to this demand. To do so would not only jeopardize England's military and imperial position in Mesopotamia, but even more importantly, it would undermine Anglo-French relations. George Clerk, head of the war department at the Foreign Office, noted on October 19 the dilemma faced by the Foreign Office:

It is difficult to challenge the position which France claims, and has to some extent secured by acquiring special interests, in the northwestern portion [Lebanon–Syria] of Arabia as now defined by the Arabs. But we cannot win the Arabs unless we can reconcile French and Arab claims and the position must be clearly understood from both the French and the Arab side from the outset, or we shall be heading straight for serious trouble.[30]

On October 24 McMahon explained to Sherif Hussein Britain's position on the question of future Arab boundaries:

The districts of Mersina and Alexandretta and portions of Syria lying to the west of the districts of Damascus, Hama, Homs and Aleppo cannot be said to be purely Arab and should be excluded from the proposed limits and boundaries.
With the above modification, and without prejudice to our existing treaties with Arab chiefs, we accept those limits and boundaries, and in regard to those portions of the territories wherein Great Britain is free to act without detriment to her Ally, France. I am empowered in the name of the Government of Great Britain to give you the following assurances and make the following reply to your letter:
Subject to the above modifications, Great Britain is prepared to recognize and support the independence of the Arabs within the territories included in the limits and boundaries proposed by the Sherif of Mecca.
Great Britain will guarantee the Holy Places against all external aggression and will recognize their inviolability.
When the situation admits, Great Britain will give to the Arabs her advice and will assist them to establish what may appear to be the most suitable forms of government in those various territories.
On the other hand, it is understood that the Arabs have decided to seek the advice and assistance of Great Britain only, and that such European advisers and officials as may be required in the formation of a sound form of administration will be British.
With regard to the Vilayets of Baghdad and Basra, the Arabs will recognize that the established position and interests of Great Britain necessitates special measures of administrative control in order to secure these territories from foreign aggression, to promote the wel-

---

[25] Report by Saint-Quentin, "Visées anglaises sur la Syrie," to Millerand, July 28, 1915, Archives Marine, carton Ea 199, pp. 8–10.

[26] Paul Cambon, French ambassador to Great Britain, to Grey, Aug. 31, 1915, AAE, série: Guerre 1914–1918, vol. 870, fol. 81. The Viviani Cabinet governed from August, 1914, to October, 1915.

[27] Delcassé to P. Cambon, Aug. 24, 1915, ibid., fol. 39. See also Defrance to Delcassé, July 30, 1915, ibid., vol. 869, fol. 158.

[28] Aristide Briand, French premier, to P. Cambon, Nov. 13, 1915, ibid., vol. 871, fol. 48; Colonel Panouse, French military attaché to Great Britain, to General Pierre Roques, French war minister, Nov. 13, 26, 1915, AMG, 7N 2170, dossier 530; Colonel Joseph Girodin to Roques, Nov. 14, 1915, ibid.

[29] The details of the negotiations are discussed in Kedourie, 1976: chaps. ii–iii. See also A. L. Tibawi, *A Modern History of Syria Including Lebanon and Palestine* (London, 1969), pp. 209–235.

[30] Clerk, Minutes, Oct. 19, 1915, F.O. 371/2468, 34982/15290.

fare of the local populations and to secure our mutual economic interests.

The Sherif replied on November 5 that "we renounce our insistence on the inclusion of the *wilāyas* of Mersina and Adana in the Arab Kingdom. But the two *wilāyas* of Aleppo and Beirut and their sea coasts are purely Arab *wilāyas*." To which McMahon on December 14 reaffirmed his previous position that French interests were paramount:

With regard to the *vilayets* of Aleppo and Beirut, the Government of Great Britain have fully understood and taken careful note of your observations, but, as the interests of our ally, France, are involved in them both, the question will require careful consideration and a further communication on the subject will be addressed to you in due course.[31]

At no time did McMahon and Hussein agree to the boundaries of the proposed Arab state.

McMahon thought that he had discovered the means by which British, French, and Arab claims could be reconciled. His letter of October 24 was remarkably clear concerning British postwar prerogatives in Mesopotamia, Arabia, and the future Arab state. Unfortunately, McMahon was ambiguous when he described Hussein's reward. Ostensibly McMahon had promised Hussein an independent Arab state, one that included Syria. But this promise of an independent Arab state, as McMahon told Hussein on October 24 and December 14, was limited to those territories where France had no claims. France, however, claimed Lebanon, Syria, and Palestine; thus, the future Arab state would have to be confined to the Arabian peninsula. Furthermore, no mention was made of the form which Arab independence would take nor of the nature of the autonomous governments established in the various districts concerned.

McMahon realized that his famous October 24 letter could have been clearer. At least possible future French claims had been protected. He wrote Grey:

I have been definite in stating that Great Britain will recognize the principle of Arab independence in purely Arab territory, this being the main point on which agreement depends, but have been equally definite in excluding Mersina, Alexandretta and those districts on the northern coast of Syria, which cannot be said to be Arab, and where I understand that French interests have been recognized. I am not aware of the extent of French claims in Syria, nor of how far His Majesty's Government have agreed to recognize them. Hence, while recognizing the towns of Damascus, Hama, Homs and Aleppo as being within the circle of Arab countries, I have endeavoured to provide for possible French pretensions to those places by a general modification to the effect that His Majesty's Government can only give assurances in regard to those territories "in which she can act without detriment to the interests of her ally France."[32]

Although he had followed Foreign Office directives and had provided for future French "pretensions," McMahon realized that Anglo-Arab relations would greatly improve if France would vanish from the Middle East:

I venture to emphasize the fact that the eventual arrangement would be very greatly facilitated if France would consent to forego any territorial claims she may have to purely Arab territories, such as Damascus, Hama, Homs and Aleppo. The inclusion of such districts in Arabia will be insisted on by the Arabs, and although they might possibly agree in regard to them to accept from France a similar arrangement to that which we are proposing elsewhere, it is obvious that this will give rise to trouble, and that much more satisfactory and lasting results will be possible in the future if the Arab question can be dealt with as a whole by Great Britain.
In face of the vital importance to the Allied cause of the present issues involved, France could hardly be unreasonable on this point and the question of compensation elsewhere if necessary is well worthy of serious consideration.
It is, I consider, not going too far to say that the only hope of preventing this question becoming eventually one of trouble and anxiety to all concerned is to leave it in the direction of one power alone.[33]

But France's claims to Syria and Lebanon would not disappear. Nor could Britain "buy the French out"[34] by swapping Nigeria for Syria.[35] Thus the Foreign Office decided to consult France and to determine France's specific interests in the Levant.

On October 21, 1915, Edward Grey obliquely asked Paris to send a representative to London in order to discuss "the Syrian borders."[36] France was aware that Arab nationalists had contacted England and offered to lead a revolt against Turkey if England were to recognize an independent Arab kingdom stretching from the Persian Gulf to the Mediterranean. It was thought by French officials that England would never pay the price:

If Syria's possible destiny [under French control] were not enough to make them [British] reject the condition put forth by [the Nationalists], the [British] desire to preserve the lands in Iraq already conquered or to be conquered would certainly impel them [British] to reject

---

[31] The letters are quoted in Kedourie, 1976: pp. 97–115.

[32] McMahon to Grey, Oct. 26, 1915, F.O. 371/2486, 34982/163832.

[33] *Ibid.*

[34] Lieutenant Colonel A. C. Parker, assigned to the War Office, to General Gilbert Clayton, director of British Military Intelligence in Cairo, Nov. 18, 1915, F.O. 882/16, fol. 193.

[35] Aubrey Herbert, a member of Parliament who served in Gallipoli and Cairo, to Grey, Oct. 30, 1915, F.O. 371/2486, 34982/16459.

[36] P. Cambon to Viviani, Oct. 21, 1915, AAE, série: A Paix, vol. 128.

at any price the overtures which have been made to them.³⁷

France also knew that Great Britain had been attempting to persuade Hussein to rebel against the Turks. France thought that the extent of British promises to Hussein included an independent state within the Arabian peninsula. The Quai d'Orsay realized that such a future Arabian state could be contiguous to Syria. Grey's offer to clarify the Syrian boundaries made sense.³⁸ But there was another factor, one that overjoyed Paris and greatly enticed it to accept the British offer quickly: France thought that the offer to discuss the Syrian borders was England's "first official recognition of [French] rights in Syria." Consequently, the newly established government of Aristide Briand immediately appointed François Georges-Picot to represent France in the forthcoming Middle East discussions.³⁹

Picot's selection was no surprise. He had been France's prewar consul at Beirut, transferred to Cairo when the war erupted, and was currently serving in London as first secretary of the French embassy. Picot was a strong advocate of French overseas expansion. His views were supported by French public opinion, powerful commercial interests, important segments of the military establishment, and colonial pressure groups in parliament.⁴⁰ Most importantly, Picot represented the colonial mentality that pervaded France's cabinets and foreign service for the period 1914–1920. French imperialism in the Middle East was supported by Victor Augagneur, minister of the navy in the Viviani government; Maurice Paléologue, ambassador to Russia; Paul Cambon, ambassador to England; Jules-Albert Defrance, ambassador to Egypt; Robert de Caix, adviser to the Quai d'Orsay on Middle Eastern affairs; Jean Goût, chief of the Asian department at the Quai d'Orsay; Georges Leygues, minister of the navy in the Clemenceau government; Stéphen Pichon, minister of foreign affairs in the Clemenceau Cabinet from late 1917 to January, 1920; Bruno de Margerie, chief of the commercial and political division at the Quai d'Orsay during the war; Philippe Berthelot, Margerie's assistant, Briand's *chef du cabinet,* and then appointed in 1919 chief of the commercial and political division at the Quai d'Orsay; Alexandre Ribot, premier and minister of foreign affairs during much of 1917; and Alexandre Millerand, war minister in the Viviani Cabinet, and premier in 1920.⁴¹

Picot received specific instructions from Premier Briand. Picot was to win British approval for French postwar claims to Syria. Briand defined Syria much as his immediate predecessors had done, that is, the territory stretching from the Egyptian frontier north to the Taurus mountain range and from there east to the Persian border. How could France justify the seizure of such a large area, one that included not only Arabs but a sizable number of Turks, Armenians, and Kurds? Briand was convinced that the Ottoman Empire would not survive the postwar peace conference. Russia had been promised Constantinople, Italy a slice of western Anatolia, and British troops were in Mesopotamia heading northward and no one knew where they would stop. Compared to other European powers, France would be the biggest loser if the Turkish empire collapsed. French involvement in Turkey's prewar economy had been unrivaled by any European country. France had administered the Public Debt and controlled the Imperial Ottoman Bank. French capital had bought the Turkish loans and built many of the railways, roads, ports, and harbors. Briand considered his demand for postwar control of an enlarged Syria to be a reasonable request in the sense that France would be compensated for the loss of her privileged prewar position within the Ottoman Empire.⁴²

On November 23, 1915, Picot met the British representatives led by Sir Arthur Nicolson, permanent undersecretary of state for foreign affairs. Picot had gone to London to discuss the boundaries of a French-controlled Syria.⁴³ He quickly discovered that England had other plans. Nicolson explained that in order to encourage Hussein to rebel, England and France would have to offer him more territory. Although France could have direct control of Lebanon, Nicolson requested that Syria, including the major towns of Damascus, Aleppo, Homs, and Hama, be given to Hussein. Thereupon Syria, Mesopotamia, and the Hejaz could either form a confederation or unite into a single Arab state. France, however, would have a sphere of interest in Syria. France would be given exclusive economic and political rights in Syria. Whereas "nominal sovereignty [would be] accorded the Arabs," France, according to Nicolson, would have "all the real benefits of the

---

³⁷ Defrance to Viviani, Oct. 28, 1915, Archives Marine, carton Ea 199, dossier: Turquie, Renseignements politiques et économiques 1914–1915.

³⁸ P. Cambon to Viviani, Oct. 21, 1915, AAE, série: A Paix, vol. 128.

³⁹ Quai d'Orsay memo, "Note pour le président du conseil," Oct. 28, 1915, *ibid.* Briand, who replaced Viviani as premier in October, 1915, would govern until March, 1917.

⁴⁰ See above, pp. 6–7, esp. note 18; C. M. Andrew and A. S. Kanya-Forstner, "The French Colonial Party and French Colonial War Aims, 1914–1918," *Hist. Jour.* **17** (1974): pp. 83, 86.

⁴¹ Picot, as well as most of those listed above, were either prewar or wartime subscribers to the leading colonial journal, *L'Asie française.*

⁴² Briand to Picot, Nov. 2, 1915, AAE, série: Guerre 1914–1918, vol. 871, fols. 32–36. The Briand government was formed in November, 1915.

⁴³ Briand to P. Cambon, Nov. 9, 1915, *ibid.,* fol. 31.

governing power." [44] Three days later Nicolson explained that Syria, and not Lebanon and Palestine, "would be entrusted to the Arabs but under such conditions that France would in fact be vested with a protectorate amounting to a takeover." [45] The English balancing act over the question of Syrian sovereignty was intended to satisfy Sherif Hussein's demands for an independent Syria and French demands for a predominant role in Syria.

The basic proposals presented by Nicolson supposedly had been agreeable to Hussein and the Arab nationalists in Cairo. A few days before Picot's arrival in Paris, Sir Mark Sykes had met one of the Arab nationalists in Cairo, Sherif-al-Faruqi, and "anticipating French difficulty discussed the situation with him with that in view." Faruqi agreed that, if the Arabs were to rule Syria, Palestine, and Lebanon, France would supply the political advisers, maintain its established educational institutions, have a monopoly on all new economic enterprises, and control the railways. [46]

Picot greeted the Anglo-Arab proposals about an independent Arab state with "complete incredulity." [47] He maintained that no French government could survive politically if it surrendered French claims in Syria. Palestine, Lebanon, and Syria were "near the heart of the French and that now, after the expenditure of so many lives, France would never consent to offer independence to the Arabs." However, Picot did offer a counterproposal, one that he considered as unrealistic as the British offer: France would allow the Arabs to have a small independent state in the Mosul area if the British gave up all claims to Baghdad, Basra, and the Arabian peninsula. England rejected this proposal. With the negotiations now deadlocked, Picot returned to Paris and reported the British plans to Briand. The British were pessimistic about Briand's response. [48]

Briand was not ready to give up Syria. Nevertheless, he was not unduly upset by the British suggestions. He believed that the French bargaining position should be flexible. England, not France, was fighting in the Middle East. Briand reasoned that direct possession of Syria would entail enormous military and administrative expenses. A protectorate would be less expensive and would still allow France to control the area. France, however, would continue to demand direct control of Palestine, Lebanon, Alexandretta, Cilicia, and the regions stretching eastward from Urfa and Marash to Diarbekir and Mosul.

Briand was slightly troubled by one aspect of Nicolson's program, the problem of "double suzerainty." Syria would be under a French protectorate and still have political ties wth the Sherif of Mecca. Briand quickly dismissed this potential difficulty. It was "utopian" to think that the Arabs could create a large political state. [49] The premier was simply reflecting the sentiments of those most closely tied to the Middle Eastern negotiations. Picot believed that Arab tribal rivalries would prevent political unification. He believed that all British promises to the Arabs would never succeed. "What the British want," observed Picot, "is only to deceive the Arabs. They hope to accomplish this by offering them a lot while admitting that the building they are constructing will probably not last beyond the war." [50] Nicolson, who had asked France to recognize an independent Syrian state, privately agreed with Picot that an independent Arab state was an "absurdity" and an "impractical proposal." [51]

Precisely because the possibility of an independent Arab state was considered so remote explains why Picot returned to London and announced on December 21 that France as a "loyal ally" would abide by London's wishes. France would accept a protectorate rather than direct control of Syria. Picot then asked what territories would be placed under France's direct control. Nicolson replied that France could have the coastal territory north of Lebanon stretching to Cilicia, and then eastward to Diarbekir. France could not possess Lebanon, Mosul, or Palestine. Although allowed to have a French governor, Lebanon would be part of the future Arab confederation. Picot demanded that France have direct control of the entire coastal area north of the Egyptian frontier. The meeting ended with French protests that Lebanese Christians should not be placed under Moslem authority. [52]

During the next several days Picot met with Sir

---

[44] Meeting of Nov. 23, 1915, AAE, série: A Paix, vol. 129.

[45] P. Cambon to Briand, Nov. 26, 1915, AAE, série: Guerre 1914–1918, vol. 871, fol. 92.

[46] Sykes's letter is contained in McMahon to Grey, Nov. 21, 1915, F.O. 371/2486, 34982/175418. See also Sykes to Sir Percy Cox, at this time Chief Political Officer in Basra, Nov. 22, 1915, F.O. 882/15, fol. 61; A. Nicolson to Grey, Feb. 2, 1916, F.O. 371/2767, 938/23579.

[47] Lord Charles Hardinge, Indian viceroy, to A. Nicolson, Dec. 28, 1915, Papers of Sir Arthur Nicolson, Public Record Office, London, F.O. 800/380. Hardinge recounted the information that he received from the India Office about the November 23 meeting with Picot.

[48] Parker, who represented the War Office in the negotiations with Picot, to Clayton, Nov. 23, 1915, F.O. 882/2, fols. 156–158; Clerk, "Minutes," Dec. 1, 1915, F.O. 371/2486, 34982/181716.

[49] Briand to P. Cambon, Dec. 14, 1915, AAE, série: A Paix, vol. 129.

[50] Picot to Briand, Dec. 2, 1915, *ibid.*

[51] A. Nicolson to Hardinge (copy), Dec. 16, 1915, Nicolson Papers, F.O. 800/380.

[52] "Meeting between Sir Arthur Nicolson, Sykes . . . and Picot," Dec. 21, 1915, AAE, série: Guerre, 1914–1918, vol. 871, fols. 117–120; P. Cambon to Briand, Dec. 22, 1915, *ibid.*, fols. 121–123; Arab Bureau memo, "Results of Third Meeting of Committee to Discuss the Syrian Question . . . 21st December 1915," F.O. 882/16, fols. 215–217.

Mark Sykes, England's new chief negotiator. The two men quickly and easily settled the outstanding differences. Britain claimed Palestine. France resisted, and it was agreed that Palestine would be placed under an international administration. France was given direct control of Lebanon, while Mosul and additional territory stretching to the Persian border were placed in the Arab zone, where France would have the dominant sphere of interest. In return, England received complete possession of the Palestine ports of Haifa and Acre. England also received the exclusive right to build and administer a railway connecting Haifa with Mesopotamia. Briand would have preferred joint Anglo-French control of Haifa and the proposed railway. Both Briand and Picot agreed that French intransigence would jeopardize "the considerable advantages already won."[53] The premier was correct. Without these concessions there would have been no agreement. British imperial interests in Persia, India, and Mesopotamia dictated that England have control of both a Mediterranean port and a railway to the east.[54]

All of the Anglo-French agreements of the past six weeks were incorporated in a January 3, 1916, memorandum signed by Picot and Sykes. The most important provisions dealt with the areas of direct control and the protectorate regions. The clauses dealing with the areas of direct control were quite clear. The French zone—designated the blue area—ran north of Palestine to Cilicia and then eastward to the Persian border. The British zone—designated the red area—covered the head of the Persian Gulf. In these areas France and Great Britain were free "to establish such direct or indirect administration or control as they desire."

The clauses covering the protectorate areas were a bit murky. The two countries agreed "to recognize and protect an independent State or a Confederation of Arab states . . . under the suzerainty of an Arab chief." The Arab state or confederation would be divided into a northern area under French protection—designated "A" (approximately modern day Syria)—and a southern area under English protection—designated "B." In area "A" France and in area "B" Britain were to "have priority of rights of enterprise and local loans . . . and . . . alone supply advisers or foreign functionaries at the request of the Arab state or Confederation of Arab States."[55] What was the relationship between France and zone "A"? According to his latest biographer, Sykes believed that, except for the coastal area, the agreement "denied Syria to France."[56] Yet only a few months following the signing of the 1916 agreement Sykes told the British government that the Arabs would resist "any pretensions which the French may see fit to put forward in regard to Syria at a later date."[57] Sykes may have believed that the recent agreement served as the basis of French "pretensions." British officials at the India Office certainly thought so. They feared that the agreement would give the French "domination" in area "A," Syria.[58] The French obviously thought that they were getting a protectorate over area "A." France would be permitted to "protect" the state or confederation of states comprising area "A." This implied that French troops would be the dominant military force in area "A." Nothing was stipulated about when and against whom French troops could be used. Certainly France, with her "priority of rights of enterprise and local loans" would control the economic life of the area. France would also supply the technicians and political and economic advisers, but "only at the request of the Arab state." Suppose the future Arab state or confederation did not invite the French advisers? This question of sovereignty disturbed at least one adviser at the Quai d'Orsay. After all, how could an Arab state be "independent" and under French control at the same time? The French official maintained that the best way to assure French influence in area "A" was to clarify the agreement. It was imperative that "the appointment of the Emir or the Emirs of Damascus and Aleppo by France be stated explicitly; without this our influence would be an illusion."[59] This was not done.

The vagueness of the agreement did not concern Briand and Picot. Precision on the question of where sovereignty lay in the future Arab state was not needed when Briand believed that such a state could never be created. If it were created, it would be powerless to resist French pressure. Briand, however, did have an uneasy feeling about France's future in the Middle East. The source of his anxiety came from London, not Damascus or Mecca:

We must take all precautions against any possibility of a partial fulfillment of the agreement [January 3 memorandum] benefiting for example the English, should circumstances allow them to occupy their share and to achieve their objective without France being in a posi-

---

[53] Briand, "Négociations franco-anglaises," Jan. 2–3(?), 1916, AAE, série: A Paix, vol. 129. See also Picot to P. Cambon, Jan. 3, 1916, AAE, série: Guerre 1914–1918, vol. 871, fols. 149–154.
[54] Parker (?), "Note on the Syrian Question," Dec. 27, 1915, F.O. 882/16, fols. 218–220.
[55] Memorandum, Jan. 4, 1916, AAE, série: Guerre 1914–1918, vol. 871, fols. 159–160.

[56] Roger Adelson, *Mark Sykes: Portrait of an Amateur* (London, 1975), p. 201.
[57] Sykes, Memo to War Committee, Oct. 14, 1916, F.O. 371/2775, 42233/203311.
[58] Adelson, 1975: p. 201.
[59] Unsigned Quai d'Orsay memo, early Jan., 1916, AAE, série: A Paix, vol. 129.

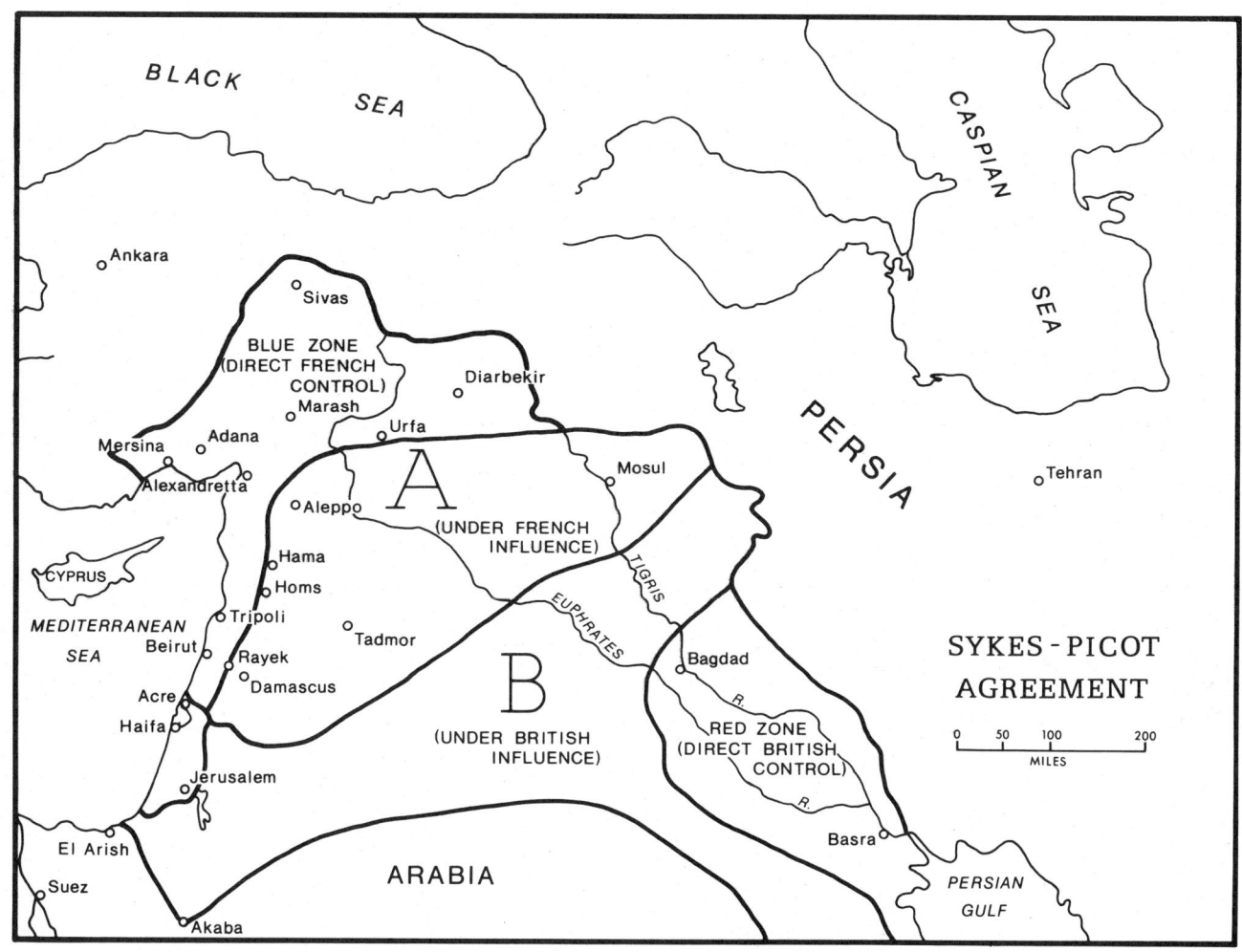

MAP. 1. Sykes-Picot agreement.

tion to take possession of her share of sovereignty [blue zone] and influence [zone "A"].[60]

In the following few weeks the French and British governments agreed upon some relatively insignificant additions to the January 3 memorandum. In early February the two governments tentatively approved this memorandum. This would later be known as the Sykes-Picot agreement.[61] The agreement was not formally approved by the two governments until the spring of 1916 since Russia's approval was needed.[62] Russia consented—but for a price.

The eastern portion of France's blue zone was given to Russia. In addition, Russia was to receive Turkish territory to the northeast of the French zone. France, in turn, was "compensated." The blue zone was expanded northward, at Turkey's expense, to Sivas.[63]

---

[60] Briand to P. Cambon, Jan. 5, 1916, *ibid.*

[61] Briand to P. Cambon, Feb. 8, 1916, *ibid.*; memorandum approved by the English Cabinet, Feb. 7 (?), 1916, *ibid.*; Quai d'Orsay memo, "Négociations de Paul Cambon et de Georges-Picot sur la Syrie," Jan. 31, 1916, AAE, série: Guerre 1914–1918, vol. 871, fol. 22.

[62] The Sykes-Picot agreement is contained in the letter from Lord Grey to Paul Cambon, May 16, 1916, Great Britain, Foreign Office, Historical Section, *Documents on British Foreign Policy, 1919–1939*, E. L. Woodward and Rohan Butler, eds. (13 v., London, 1947–1963; hereafter cited as

BD), 1st series, vol. 4, pp. 245–247. See Appendix I for the agreement in its entirety.

[63] Serge Sazonov, Russian minister of foreign affairs, to Paléologue, Apr. 26, 1916, AMG, 6N 197, dossier: Engagements anglais-Picot Accords; Grey to McMahon, Apr. 27, 1916, F.O. 371/2768, 938/76954.

For different interpretations of the Sykes-Picot agreement, see Briton Cooper Busch, *Britain, India, and the Arabs, 1914–1921* (Berkeley, 1971), pp. 81–88; Isaiah Friedman, *The Question of Palestine, 1914–1918: British-Jewish-Arab Relations* (London, 1973), chap. vii; Comte Roger de Gontaut-Biron, *Comment la France s'est installée en Syrie, 1918–1919* (Paris, 1922), chap. ii; Elie Kedourie, *England and the Middle East: The Destruction of the Ottoman Empire* (London, 1956), chap. ii; Jukka Nevakivi, *Britain, France and the Arab Middle East, 1914–1920* (London, 1969), pp. 30–44; Jean Pichon, *Le Partage du Proche-Orient* (Paris, 1938), chap. vi; Leonard Stein, *The Balfour Declaration* (New York, 1961), chap. xvi; Tibawi, 1969: pp. 235–240.

The Briand government considered the Sykes-Picot agreement as "definitive" and "final."[64] The agreement promised to give France a dominant position in the postwar Middle East. Seemingly only a German victory threatened the implementation of the agreement. The Arabs appeared to be no threat to the agreement. Nor, apparently, was McMahon's October 24, 1915, letter to Hussein concerning an independent Arab state. The Sherif had been told on October 24 and December 14, 1915, that the interests of France had to be considered. France had been consulted and the result was the Sykes-Picot agreement. Grey was correct when he noted three years later that there was no contradiction between the Sykes-Picot agreement and McMahon's promise:

I am surprised to see it stated that our engagements to the King of the Hedjaz are incompatible with our engagements to France about Syria. I think this statement must be most unfair to those who are responsible for making the engagements and will do increasing mischief to the reputation of British policy and good faith. My recollection is that we promised the King of the Hedjaz and the Musselman world that Arabia and the Musselman Holy Places should be an independent Musselman Kingdom. There was nothing in this to prevent our agreeing to the demand of France for the Syrian sphere of influence under the Sykes-Picot arrangement.[65]

McMahon also concurred that there was "nothing in the arrangement agreed on between France and Russia and ourselves that conflicts with any agreements made with or assurances given to Shereef and other Arab parties." Nevertheless, McMahon foresaw difficulties. He was concerned that Hussein would interpret the October 24, 1915, letter as an unconditional British pledge to support an independent Syrian state. For this reason McMahon advised that the Arabs not be told of the Sykes-Picot agreement.[66]

Potential threats to the 1916 Sykes-Picot agreement also arose elsewhere. Although Briand, Grey, and czarist Russia considered the 1916 agreement as internationally binding, British colonial officials immediately rejected this notion. General Gilbert Clayton, director of British Military Intelligence in Cairo, thought that the agreement "will serve as a useful guide." He observed that "events move and conditions change so swiftly that there can be no certainty that an agreement made today will suit the conditions of six months hence. Thus anything more than an informal and general understanding would be dangerous at the present stage."[67] David Hogarth, chief of the Arab Bureau in Cairo, hoped that "this Agreement is regarded by our Government now as a purely opportunist measure, with the mental reservation that it cannot but need considerable revision sooner or later. For it contains several features which do not promise any final solution of the Near Eastern Question." The basic defect of the agreement was that it would give France a solid foothold in the Middle East. The Arabs and Hussein, according to Hogarth, would never tolerate the French presence.[68]

The French, however, believed that the biggest immediate threat to the sanctity of the 1916 Middle East agreement came not from the Turks and the British, but from the Italians. Sidney Sonnino, Italian foreign minister, immediately protested the Sykes-Picot agreement. In mid-1916 he demanded Mersina and Adana, both of which were in France's blue zone. Briand rejected the Italian request. The French premier maintained that the province of Adalia, not Adana, had been promised to Italy in April, 1915, by the Treaty of London.[69] Sonnino responded that the Treaty of London contained two important clauses. If the Ottoman Empire were to be divided, Italy would receive an "equitable part" in the area bordering the province of Adalia. Secondly, the Allies recognized that Italy was interested in "maintaining the balance in the Mediterranean." Sonnino now wanted territory the size of France's blue zone. Such a territory would be "equitable" and would maintain the Mediterranean "balance."[70] Despite repeated warnings from Rome that Italy was thoroughly disillusioned with France's Middle Eastern policies, Briand in the autumn and winter of 1916 rejected all Italian claims to Adana and the Anatolian port city of Smyrna.[71] Additional territorial demands, the French maintained, need not be met because Italy had yet to declare war against Germany; Italy had made no contribution to the Darda-

---

[64] George Buchannen, British ambassador to Russia, to Grey, Mar. 12, 1916, Cabinet Office Papers, Public Record Office, London (hereafter cited as Cab.), 17/176.

[65] Memorandum enclosed in Grey to Arthur Balfour, British foreign secretary, Sept. 9, 1919, Lloyd George Papers, House of Lords Record Office, London, F/12/1/43.

[66] McMahon to Grey, May 4, 1916, F.O. 371/2768, 938/84855.

[67] Memo by Clayton, "Note on the Arab Question," July 5, 1916, F.O. 371/2774, 42333/134588.

[68] Hogarth to Captain Reginald Hall, director of the Intelligence Division of the Admiralty, May 3, 1916, F.O. 882/14, fol. 36.

[69] Quai d'Orsay memo, July 15, 1916, AAE, série: A Paix, vol. 130; Briand to P. Cambon, Sept. 22, 1916, *ibid*. For the Italian response to the Sykes-Picot agreement, see Albert Pingaud, "Le Partage de l'Asie-Mineure pendant la grande guerre, 1915–1917," *Revue d'histoire de la guerre mondiale* 17, 2 (1939): pp. 110–125; Sergio I. Minerbi, *L'Italie et la Palestine, 1914–1920* (Paris, 1970), pp. 23–28.

[70] Sonnino to Briand, Nov. 4, 1916, AAE, série: A Paix, vol. 130. See also the sixteen-page Quai d'Orsay memo reviewing the question of Italy and the Middle East, Nov. 15, 1916, *ibid*.

[71] Barrère to Briand, Nov. 16, Dec. 16, 1916, *ibid.;* Barrère to Briand, Jan. 27, Feb. 4, 23, Mar. 12, 1917, *ibid.*, vol. 131.

nelles campaign, and Italy was making an insignificant contribution to the Balkan campaign.[72]

In April, 1917, Sonnino, Prime Minister David Lloyd George of England, and Alexandre Ribot, France's new premier,[73] met at St. Jean de Maurienne. A compromise was finally arranged. Sonnino permitted the French to remove Constantine, the pro-German king of neutralist Greece. More importantly, Sonnino recognized the 1916 French-British-Russian agreement. In return for these concessions, Italy received a wide stretch of territory reaching from the outskirts of Mersina to north of Smyrna. The territory was divided into a green zone and a "C" zone. Italy was to have the same rights in these two zones as France would have in the blue and "A" zones.[74]

Thus by the summer of 1917 the Allies had agreed on the future of the Ottoman Empire. Apparently nothing but an Allied defeat would prevent France from having her share of the Sykes-Picot agreement.

2. THE ARABS, BRITISH, AND ZIONISTS, 1916–1918

In June, 1916, Hussein, the Sherif of Mecca, finally decided to revolt against the Turks. The sherifs of Mecca, all of whom were of the Hashemite family and claimed direct descent from the prophet Mohammed, had ruled Mecca and the Hejaz in western Arabia since the tenth century. The sherifs had the responsibility of protecting Medina and Mecca and overseeing the annual pilgrimages to the Holy Cities. Despite Hussein's special religious position and prestige, the revolt was limited to the Hejaz. The Arabs in Palestine, Lebanon, and Syria failed to rebel. A religious fanatic, Hussein was not a nationalist. He despised the modernism and atheism of the Young Turks, who wanted to reform the Ottoman Empire. Isolated within the Ottoman Empire, he feared that the Young Turks and his Arabian rivals would depose him. The weakness of his position, not the nebulous correspondence that he had with McMahon in late 1915, forced Hussein to join the British.[1]

The Sherifian revolt caught the French by surprise. The Quai d'Orsay did not know whether Hussein and the British had reached some sort of agreement concerning a future Arab state.[2] Nevertheless, France decided to support the rebellion. Subsidies were begun and a military mission of colonial Moslem troops led by Colonel Edouard Brémond was sent to Jidda.

Several reasons explain France's support for the Arab revolt. If the Sherifians could immobilize a few Turkish troops, it would be of some assistance to the Allies.[3] If the Sherifian rebellion spread into Syria, Lebanon, and Palestine, it would momentarily "liberate these provinces from Turkish persecution and prepare a French intervention."[4] France could not, in view of her pressing interests in Syria, afford to be entirely removed from the revolt. Should the Sherifians succeed without French assistance, French prestige in Moslem Syria would decline and the popularity of Great Britain would be enhanced at France's expense.[5] Perhaps the most important reason for France's immediate involvement in a militarily insignificant rebellion lay in the relationship between the Middle East and France's North African Moslem territories. The Quai d'Orsay realized that what "happens in Arabia could have the most serious repercussions in all our colonies." France would have to support the rebellion in order to have some control over it. If the Sherifian rebellion were to succeed without French influence, France would find herself confronted with a fast-spreading, pan-Islamic, and anti-Christian whirlwind roaring through North Africa.[6]

France realized that the Sherif of Mecca, as guardian of the Holy Places, had a great deal of prestige within the Moslem world. Close ties with Hussein, it was argued, would bolster support for France in Tunisia, Algeria, and Morocco. Friendship with Hussein would contrast sharply with the Turks who were laying siege to Mecca, Islam's holiest city.[7] For this reason Briand organized pilgrimages to Mecca for France's Moslem subjects. These North African Moslem communities would realize that France, "involved in an all-out war and despite all

---

[72] Briand to P. Cambon, Sept. 22, 1916, *ibid.*, vol. 130; Quai d'Orsay memo, "Note pour le président du conseil," Apr. 10, 1917, *ibid.*, vol. 131.

[73] Ribot, who replaced Briand as premier and minister of foreign affairs in March, 1917, held both positions until September, 1917. He then served until November as minister of foreign affairs in the Paul Painlevé Cabinet.

[74] Ribot to Paléologue, Apr. 19, 1917, AAE, série: A Paix, vol. 131. For the entire St. Jean de Maurienne agreement, the details of which were worked out over a period of several weeks, see Tommasco Tittoni, Italian ambassador to France, to Ribot, Aug. 21, 1917, AMG, 6N 197, dossier: Engagements anglais-Picot Accords.

[1] C. Ernest Dawn, *From Ottomanism to Arabism: Essays on the Origins of Arab Nationalism* (Champaign, 1973), chap. i; Elie Kedourie, *The Chatham House Version and Other Middle-Eastern Studies* (New York, 1970), p. 23.

[2] Defrance to Briand, July 5, 1916, AAE, série: Guerre 1914–1918, vol. 1682, fol. 26.

[3] War Ministry memo, Aug. 5, 1916, AMG, 7N 2140, dossier: Mission française en Egypte.

[4] *Ibid.*

[5] Quai d'Orsay memo, July 31, 1916, AAE, série: Guerre 1914–1918, vol. 1683, fol. 60; Defrance to Briand, Aug. 18, 1916, *ibid.*, vol. 1684, fol. 46.

[6] Memo by Bruno de Margerie, chief of Quai d'Orsay commercial and political division, "Note pour le président du conseil," July 19, 1916, *ibid.*, vol. 1682, fol. 185.

[7] Quai d'Orsay memo, "Rapport à M. le Président de la République," Nov. 14, 1916, *ibid.*, vol. 1688, fol. 266; War Ministry memo, Aug. 5, 1916, AMG, 7N 2140, dossier: Mission française en Egypte.

kinds of difficulties, felt herself obliged to aid her subjects ... in fulfilling one of the religious practices on which they set the most value." [8]

Why this interest in the morale of her North African subjects? France believed that the possibility of a Holy War was always present. Secondly, France wanted to counter German support of Moslem national independent movements.[9] Lastly, Briand realized that as the war dragged on, greater demands would be made on the colonies, and the colonies would have to supply more troops and more industrial laborers. These considerations explain Briand's grave concern when the Sherifian revolt appeared in danger of collapse in late 1916. After giving wide publicity in North Africa to her support of Hussein, France feared that a Sherifian defeat "would be considered in the Moslem world like a defeat for the Entente." If the Turks regained Mecca, there could be "repercussions within the Moslem communities" of French North Africa.[10]

In late 1916 there were some French officials who saw the Sherifian movement as a potential danger to France's position in the Middle East. Colonel Brémond reported from Jidda that Arab nationalists were beginning to cluster around Hussein, and their influence could be dangerous. Brémond suggested that France send someone to Jidda in order to "guide" Hussein.[11] The French ambassador to Egypt, Jules-Albert Defrance, reasoned that, if Hussein's forces broke out of Mecca, moved north, and took the Hejaz's second major city, Medina, the next stop would be Syria. Defrance recommended that Hussein be confined to Mecca for the duration of the war. France could then use Medina as "an article of exchange with [Hussein] in order to obtain his support for us in Syria." If Hussein were to reach Syria, it "would risk putting him in conflict with us." [12]

Briand rejected these suggestions. He believed that the Sherifians could not possibly reach Syria; Hussein could not even defeat Arabian chieftains such as Ibn Saud.[13] Paul Cambon, the French ambassador to Great Britain, supported Briand's assessment. Cambon argued that Hussein should be encouraged to take Syria. Such an incentive would serve to bolster the pathetic Sherifian army. In truth, Cambon did not expect the Sherifians to drive the Turks out of Arabia, let alone reach Syria. He observed that if the creation of a large Arab state were a myth "it does not behoove us to say so." [14]

French Intelligence reports in late 1916 and early 1917 substantiated the Briand government's position. The Sherifian movement was attracting an ever increasing number of Arab nationalists who wanted to gain control of Syria before France did. Inadequate military equipment and intense tribal divisions, it was thought, would prevent the Pan-Arabs from achieving their goal.[15] Unless England or France were to create an Arab empire, the Arabs would remain nothing more than a group of squabbling tribes.[16]

No matter what the Briand government thought of the military significance of the Arab revolt, Hussein in the spring of 1917 had not yet been crushed. The English Sinai offensive in early 1917 had succeeded in relieving heavy Turkish pressure on Mecca. Thus when Alexandre Ribot became premier in March, 1917, he formulated France's Middle Eastern policy based on the Sykes-Picot agreement and on the probability that Hussein would survive the war and become the leading religious figure of the Arab world.

Ribot expected postwar France to annex Lebanon and the remainder of the blue area in the Sykes-Picot agreement. There was no role for Hussein to play in the blue zone. However, there was a place for Hussein in zone "A" of the Sykes-Picot agreement, that area that had been reserved for French influence yet had also been set aside for an Arab state or confederation of states under the suzerainty of an Arab chief. Ribot believed that each of the major towns within zone "A," such as Damascus, Mosul, and Aleppo, would have an emir. This confederation of emirates would have some vague religious ties with the Sherif of Mecca. While Hussein possessed the religious power, France would possess exclusive political and economic privileges in these sheikdoms.[17]

---

[8] Briand to Gabriel-Ferdinand Alapetite, French resident-general of Tunis, Aug. 12, 1916, AMG 7N 2140, dossier: Pélérinage. See also Quai d'Orsay memo, "Rapport à M. le Président de la République," Nov. 14, 1916, AAE, série: Guerre 1914–1918, vol. 1688, fol. 266.

[9] Briand to Defrance, May 16, June 9, 1916, AAE, série: Guerre 1914–1918, vol. 1656, fols. 137, 154; Defrance to Briand, Aug. 5, 1916, ibid., vol. 1657, fol. 42.

[10] Briand to P. Cambon, Oct. 5, 1916, ibid., vol. 1686, fol. 208. See also Quai d'Orsay memo, "Note," Dec. 6, 1916, ibid., vol. 1690, fol. 102.

[11] Briand to P. Cambon, Oct. 24, 1916, AMG, 7N 2138, dossier: Mission militaire française en Egypte; Brémond to Briand, Oct. 30, Dec. 11, 1916, AAE, série: Guerre 1914–1918, vol. 1704, fols. 70, 111.

[12] Defrance to Briand, Oct. 18, 1916, AAE, série: Guerre 1914–1918, vol. 1687, fol. 124.

[13] Briand to P. Cambon, Oct. 24, 1916, AMG, 7N 2138, dossier: Mission militaire française en Egypte.

[14] P. Cambon to Briand, Nov. 24, 1916, AAE, série: Guerre 1914–1918, vol. 1689, fol. 247bis.

[15] Naval Intelligence report, Mar., 1917, ibid., vol. 1703.

[16] Report by Doynel de Saint-Quentin, Dec. 11, 1916, AMG, 7N 2140, dossier: Mouvement arabe. See also War Ministry memo, "Note sur le mouvement arabe," Feb. 13, 1917, ibid.

[17] Ribot to Mustapha Cherchali, who was in charge of French pilgrimages to Mecca, May 1, 1917, ibid., dossier: Arabie; Ribot to P. Cambon, May 22, 1917, ibid., dossier: Mission française en Egypte.

Ribot's plans clearly required Hussein's cooperation. Ribot hoped to persuade Hussein to collaborate with France. First, Ribot promptly reduced French military and technical aid to Hussein. Now that Turkey no longer threatened Mecca, France had "no motive in wishing for too rapid a development of the Sherif's military power. He would thereby become too confident and his ambitions would grow without perhaps increasing his gratitude for us."[18] The military difficulties that Hussein would encounter as a result of reduced assistance "can only serve our [French] interests by making him [Hussein] feel the limit of his strength—a limit that the Pan-Arab entourage of the king tends to underrate too much."[19] It was hoped that a more pliable Hussein would quickly understand that the road to an Arab confederation came from Paris.

Next Ribot decided to "forewarn" Hussein "of the plots by some Syrian Arabs who are already dreaming of reconstructing the Empire of the early Caliphs." If Hussein were to follow the plans of the Arab nationalists, there could be serious repercussions: "When the truth [Sykes-Picot agreement] is suddenly revealed to them [nationalists], they will make us responsible for the failure of their daydreams and instead of peaceful collaboration with them we will have to act against them—perhaps even with arms."[20] In order to eliminate any misunderstanding between France and Hussein, Ribot sent Picot to the Sherif. The purpose of the spring, 1917, visit was to win Hussein's support for the Sykes-Picot agreement and his consent to participate in Ribot's plans for the postwar Middle East.[21]

At first glance, the speed with which the Ribot government dispatched Picot to the Hejaz may seem surprising. In the spring of 1917, France was suffering great wartime military disasters on the Western Front. Despite the traumatic experience of the Nivelle defeat, military mutinies, and spreading industrial strikes, the Quai d'Orsay believed that France

must not lose sight of our interests on the Eastern shores of the Mediterranean. In view of Italian jealousy and of the intrigues of some [British] colonial officers, it is absolutely necessary that we affirm our power and that we do it immediately.[22]

If Picot were to win Hussein's support for the Sykes-Picot agreement, France's postwar position in the Middle East would have been greatly strengthened.

In late April, Picot met Sykes in Cairo. Sykes's function was to introduce Picot to Hussein. On May 19 and 20 Picot and Sykes met Hussein in Jidda. Instead of clarifying France's postwar role in Syria and Lebanon, the two-day conference led to further confusion and, eventually, tragedy. No formal minutes of the meetings were kept, with the result that the major participants never agreed to what was said. The speeches were poorly translated. Hussein could not hear everything that was said.[23] When Hussein spoke, others were mystified The king had "learned . . . to use speech to conceal his honest purpose." "Ambiguity," T. E. Lawrence recalled, "covered his every communication."[24] Sykes and Picot were not much better. Both were fast-shuffle dealers who would demonstrate once again that they were not strangers to the art of planned ambiguity.

Picot, at the meeting of May 19, referred to the 1916 agreement and told King Hussein that France wanted Lebanon and the blue area just as England intended to take Baghdad and the red area. Hussein rejected this proposal. He intended to rule Lebanon and Syria. He agreed with his chief minister who had told the British several weeks earlier that Lebanon was the "heart of Syria."[25] Hussein, however, offered France the opportunity to supply the technicians needed for the development of postwar Syria. Sykes quickly entered the discussion and insisted that the foreign advisers possess executive powers. Hussein refused. The meeting ended with no agreement.

At the second meeting, held on May 20, Hussein's foreign minister announced that France at the postwar peace conference should treat "Moslem Syria" as England intended to treat Baghdad. Picot agreed to the statement and immediately cabled Ribot that Hussein had given France a major concession.[26] Ribot congratulated Picot for having "firmly removed King Hussein's objections towards our action in Syria." But Ribot was concerned by an important problem, the meaning of the term "Moslem Syria." The term was foreign to the 1916 agreement. Apparently, "Moslem Syria" could not refer to France's blue zone, since that was predominantly Christian. Did "Moslem Syria" refer to area "A" of the Sykes-Picot agreement? If so, asked Ribot, how could "Moslem Syria" be equated with Baghdad? Bagh-

---

[18] Ribot to Paul Painlevé, French war minister, Apr. 25, 1917, AMG, 7N 2142, dossier: 1917.
[19] Ribot to P. Cambon, Apr. 7, 1917, AAE, série: Guerre 1914–1918, vol. 1695, fol. 12.
[20] Quai d'Orsay memo, "Note," Apr. 5, 1917, *ibid.*, vol. 1694, fols. 279–280.
[21] Ribot to Balfour, May 16, 1917, Lord Curzon Papers, India Office Records, London, F 112/277.
[22] Quai d'Orsay memo, May 1, 1917, AAE, série: Guerre 1914–1918, vol. 877, fol. 1.

[23] "Note by Sheilh Fuad El Khatib taken down by Lt. Col. Newcombe," June, 1917, F.O. 882/16, fol. 132; Wingate to Balfour, Aug. 16, 1917, F.O. 371/3054, 86526/174974.
[24] T. E. Lawrence, *Seven Pillars of Wisdom* (London, 1975), p. 100.
[25] Hogarth to Clayton, Feb. 12, 1917, F.O. 882/6, fol. 184.
[26] Picot to Ribot, May 24, 1917, AAE, série: Guerre 1914–1918, vol. 877, fols. 122–127. For the British involvement in these negotiations, see Kedourie, 1976: chap. v.

dad was in the red area and was to have been annexed by England. It did not make sense for a leader of a rebellion to ask an outside power to annex the territory for which he was fighting and hoped to rule.[27]

Picot responded on June 8 that, although Baghdad had been included in the red area of the Sykes-Picot agreement, Britain was not going to annex the city. Instead, Britain was going to treat Baghdad as if it were to be part of area "B," that is, part of the proposed Arab state.[28]

Why the change? Without consulting the Quai d'Orsay and the British Foreign Office, Sykes had told Hussein that Baghdad, for all intents and purposes, would be "entirely his."[29] Once Hussein knew this, as he did on the eve of the May 20 meeting, he could very easily equate Britain's position at Baghdad with France's position in "Moslem Syria."[30]

What did "Moslem Syria" mean? For Hussein this meant Syria and Lebanon. He believed that when Picot agreed to the king's May 20 statement, France was giving up all claims to Syria and Lebanon.[31] What did Picot think "Moslem Syria" meant? After all, he had agreed to equate the status of Baghdad with "Moslem Syria." Picot was not sure. He told Ribot:

Regarding the expression "Moslem Syria" which is used there, although it is possible that it may cause some ambiguity, I would see serious disadvantages in trying to clarify it now. If some day we intend to take advantage of our agreements relating to Asia Minor, we certainly shall be led sooner or later to occupy Beirut and the coast. Everything will then be easy for us as now for the English, for the Arabs always bend when confronted with a fait accompli and they candidly confessed this to me again several times during my recent trip.
On the other hand, to try to examine the question theoretically now, we run the risk of provoking an unfavorable response from the king of the Hejaz. . . .[32]

Ribot was angry. Picot spoke of "concessions," yet he had agreed to Hussein's statement without knowing what the term "Moslem Syria" entailed. Ribot feared that, if the Arab revolt spread into Syria, the Arabs would interpret "Moslem Syria" to include Christian Lebanon. If this were to occur, the premier foresaw a clash with the Arabs.[33]

The British alone seem to have benefited from the confusion surrounding the Jidda meeting. General Clayton, chief of British Intelligence in Cairo, noted a month after the meeting that the question of Syria "is at present in a state of flux and depends entirely on various developments in the war. It is therefore quite impossible to lay down anything in the least definite and all we can do is to keep the various factions in play as far as possible until the situation becomes more clear."[34] Sykes's lies to Hussein concerning the future status of Baghdad and Picot's acquiescence to the imprecision surrounding the term "Moslem Syria" were the key events in perpetuating the king's illusions about an independent Syria and Lebanon. Consequently, the Arab revolt was still "in play."

All further attempts by France to nurture a closer understanding with Hussein failed. And for good reason. England insisted that France terminate all attempts to influence Hussein. When France announced in August, 1916, that it would send a military mission to the Hejaz, England questioned the necessity of such a mission.[35] It was feared that "politically [England] shall have to pay a very high price for all material assistance the French give the Sherif."[36] France assured England that the mission, led by Colonel Brémond, had a strictly military purpose and would not interfere in the political and economic life of the Hejaz;[37] Brémond was instructed "to act only in full accord with the English."[38] However, in the ensuing months Brémond attempted to foster a pro-French clique within Hussein's entourage.[39] He also urged that greater trade be undertaken between the Hejaz and France's North African states. In addition, he strongly recommended that water and agricultural experts from France's Moslem territories be sent to the Hejaz.[40]

---

[27] Ribot to Picot, May 29, 1917, AAE, série: Guerre 1914–1918, vol. 877, fol. 150.
[28] Picot to Ribot, June 8, 1917, ibid., fol. 186.
[29] "Note by Sheilh Fuad El Khatib taken down by Lt. Col. Newcombe," June, 1917, F.O. 882/16, fol. 134.
[30] Kedourie, 1976: pp. 177–180. The British delegation at Jidda was stunned and disgusted by Sykes's action. His promise to Hussein was repudiated. The British had no intention of giving Baghdad complete independence (Colonel C. E. Wilson, British military representative in Jidda, to Clayton, May 24, 1917, F.O. 882/16, fols. 106–111).
[31] Captain T. E. Lawrence, Note of July 30, 1917, F.O. 882/12, fol. 262.
[32] Picot to Ribot, June 8, 1917, AAE, série: Guerre 1914–1918, vol. 877, fols. 187–188.
[33] Ribot to Picot, June 11, 1917, ibid., fol. 208.
[34] Clayton to Wilson, June 26, 1917, F.O. 882/16, fols. 129–130.
[35] P. Cambon to Briand, Aug. 25, 1916, AAE, série: Guerre 1914–1918, vol. 1684, fols. 137–138.
[36] General A. Murray, commander of the Egyptian Expeditionary Forces, to General William Robertson, chief of the Imperial British Army, Sept. 6, 1916, F.O. 371/2779, 152849/178902.
[37] P. Cambon to Briand, Aug. 25, 1916, AAE, série: Guerre 1914–1918, vol. 1684, fols. 137–138.
[38] Briand to Brémond, Aug. 20, 1916, Archives Marine, carton Ea 200, dossier: 1916–1917.
[39] Lieutenant de Vaisseau Louis Guichard, "Les Forces navales françaises en Syrie, Egypte, Mer Rouge, 1914–1918," Service historique de l'Etat-Major de la Marine, n.d., Bibliothèque Historique des Archives Centrales de la Marine, Château de Vincennes, Vincennes, p. 619.
[40] Brémond to Briand, Oct. 19, 1916, AAE, série: Guerre 1914–1918, vol. 1704, fol. 48; Brémond to Ribot, May 25, 1917, ibid., vol. 1706.

When in May, 1917, Ribot asked Hussein about the possibility of establishing a bank in Jidda so that France's Moslem pilgrims could be assured of "a serious and honest financial institution," [41] London responded. England had been afraid that once a French bank were established in Jidda, King Hussein would be encouraged to borrow at very low rates. Once in debt, the king would succumb to French political influence.[42] When Ribot's plans became known, London requested that the French mission be recalled.[43]

Ribot responded that he would reduce the French mission but only because the Turkish threat to Mecca had dissipated. But he wanted political and economic equality with England in the Hejaz. The premier emphasized that France's Moslem population would never permit England, a Christian country, to have a privileged position at Mecca.[44] This harsh response brought a warning from Picot. He reminded the premier that "in this question of Hejaz, as formerly in that of Fashoda, we are clashing with a vital interest of the British empire, which feels that it can give up nothing in Arabia that it needs in order to be assured of complete possession of the route of the Indies and exclusive control of the Persian Gulf."[45]

But Ribot persisted, believing that the English "have no clear idea at all of our rights and our interests in Arabia."[46] In August, Robert Cecil, British undersecretary of state for foreign affairs bluntly told Ribot that Great Britain had dominated the Arabian peninsula for more than a century. And Britain expected to maintain her exclusive position there. Cecil warned Ribot of the "dangers which would be entailed by any attempt to internationalize Arabian politics. . . ."[47] The French premier understood. Two months later France formally recognized Britain's "special political interests in Arabia."[48]

In the autumn of 1917 the major emphasis of the Arab Revolt had shifted to Emir Feisal, Hussein's third son. The Arabs had just defeated the Turks at Akaba. Feisal was an Arab nationalist who wanted to rule Syria. England subsidized Feisal's army and Colonel T. E. Lawrence conducted his military strategy.[49] Certainly there were military reasons for British support of Feisal. But French officials in the Middle East discerned that there may be as yet unclear "political" reasons for British support of Feisal and the Arab nationalists.[50]

The immediate question for France was how to respond to Feisal and the recent Arab victories. Picot recommended that France send three divisions to the Middle East. Without this power to counter the Arabs and thus get to Damascus before Feisal did, the Sykes-Picot agreement would become a "dead letter."[51] The French government, however, could afford no more than a few thousand troops in the Middle East. France was pouring all available reserves into Italy in an attempt to save that country.[52] France thus had no alternative but to rely on England to curb Feisal. The initial results were not encouraging. In late 1917, when Ribot protested to London about the use of Lawrence and Feisal in small-scale military operations in southern Syria, Britain rejected the plea. General Edmund Allenby, newly appointed commander of the Egyptian Expeditionary Force, explained that political considerations had to be sacrificed for the common good of the campaign.[53]

The Georges Clemenceau government, assuming power in November, 1917, watched Allenby's army march through Palestine, carrying Feisal in its wake. In early 1918 Stéphen Pichon, minister of foreign affairs in Clemenceau's Cabinet, told Picot, then serving as the French representative in Palestine, to initiate discussions with Feisal. Pichon hoped that these discussions would wean Feisal away from England. Feisal could then become a French puppet.[54] Picot replied that it would be useless to begin

---

[41] Ribot to Cherchali, May 1, 1917, AMG, 7N 2140, dossier: Arabie.

[42] Captain George Lloyd, a member of Parliament who served in the British Intelligence bureau in Cairo, "Report on the Hejaz," Dec. 22, 1916, F.O. 882/6, fol. 79. See also Wilson to Clayton, Feb. 10, 1917, F.O. 882/16, fols. 48–49.

[43] Balfour to Ribot, May 13, 1917, AMG, 7N 2142, dossier: 1917.

[44] Ribot to Francis Bertie, British ambassador to Paris, May 22, 1917, AAE, série: Guerre 1914–1918, vol. 1695, fols. 312–317.

[45] Picot to Ribot, June 4, 1917, ibid., vol. 1696, fol. 62. Fashoda refers to the bitter conflict between France and England over the Sudan in the late 1890's.

[46] Ribot to P. Cambon, June 22, 1917, AMG, 7N 2140, dossier: Mission française en Egypte.

[47] Cecil to Ribot, Aug. 29, 1917, AAE, série: Guerre 1914–1918, vol. 1698, fols. 95–98.

[48] Quai d'Orsay memo, "Note au sujet de l'arrangement franco-anglais sur le Hedjaz," July, 1918, AAE, série: Levant 1918–1929, Arabie, vol. 1, fol. 194.

[49] Lawrence, 1975.

[50] Defrance to Pichon, Feb. 26, 1918, AAE, série: Guerre 1914–1918, vol. 884, fol. 57.

[51] Picot, "Note," July 19, 1917, ibid., vol. 878, fol. 78; Picot to Pichon, Nov. 29, 1917, ibid., vol. 880, fol. 101.

[52] Quai d'Orsay memo, "Note pour le ministre," Nov. 20, 1917, ibid., fol. 4.

[53] Gaston Maugras, assistant to Picot in the occupied territories of Palestine and Syria, to Picot, Oct. 14, 1917, ibid., vol. 879, fols. 74–75.

[54] Pichon to Picot, Feb. 28, 1918, ibid., vol. 884, fol. 81. The French view of Feisal had not changed very much. A year earlier, in January, 1917, Feisal was described as "a braggert. He has no scruples about inventing battles, all of them victorious; a Turkish patrol squad has only to enter an area and his partisans have spotted it and he writes and sends wires that it has been beaten and pursued. He talks a lot but says nothing. He acts little and does nothing" (report by Brémond, Jan. 2, 1917, ibid., vol. 1691, fol. 170).

negotiations with Feisal because the Arab leader "sees in us only an obstacle to be brushed aside and he will be this way until the time when we can negotiate with him while possessing some leverage."[55] With only a few troops, France as yet had no leverage. Consequently, Pichon could only adopt a wait-and-see attitude. In the meantime, he took solace in the fact that even if Feisal "succeeded in setting himself up . . . in Damascus, he could maintain his authority there only with the help of a European power; the jealousies of the chieftains and the rivalries of the tribes will soon have reduced his power to nothing if France or England do not support him." Pichon emphasized, as if to reassure himself, that if Feisal "happens to conquer Damascus, he will have to seek France as his protector."[56] Pichon's assessment of Feisal's potential ineffectiveness was based on the latest French Intelligence reports. The chief of the French Middle Eastern Intelligence network informed Paris in early 1918 that it was "absolutely impossible to create a native Syrian kingdom, even one with illusionary power." Divided into a number of "nations and nationalities, Syria, from a political point of view, was like dust." Only a selfless, disinterested European power such as France, could equitably administer the country.[57]

By 1918 Feisal and the Arab nationalists were depending upon the English army to reach Syria. Likewise France was dependent upon British military success against the Turks for the implementation of France's blueprint for the Middle East, the Sykes-Picot agreement. Some French officials were beginning to wonder if England would make the correct choice.

For the first two years of the war British forces remained on the Suez Canal. However, in late 1916 Britain began to plan a Sinai offensive. The immediate purposes of the campaign were to give greater security to the canal and to disrupt Turkish communications into Arabia, thereby assisting Hussein's rebellion. Edward Grey, British foreign secretary, fully aware that the Sykes-Picot agreement had reserved Syria for France, asked Briand in early October, 1916, whether France would be willing to attack the Turks in Syria while the English attacked in the Gaza.[58] Briand rejected a Syrian offensive. He believed that all British troops in Egypt as well as all available French troops should be sent to the Balkans in an attempt to save a collapsing Rumania.[59]

There was one aspect of Britain's plan that greatly disturbed Briand. Suppose the British were successful and continued beyond El-Arish.[60] General Archibald Murray, Allenby's predecessor as commander of the Egyptian Expeditionary Force, had told the French that, if possible, the British offensive would go as far as Alexandretta.[61] To allay French fears, Lloyd George promised Briand that, if the British reached Palestine, Picot and Sykes would control the civil administration of the area.[62] General Murray's Gaza offensive, however, was stopped by the Turks in April, 1917. The problem of Palestine was delayed.

In the late autumn of 1917 General Allenby led a successful Sinai offensive against the Turks and in December the British took Jerusalem. Picot assumed his position as high commissioner to Palestine, as had been agreed upon a year earlier. Allenby, however, refused to allow him any authority. The British general, supported by Prime Minister Lloyd George, claimed that Jerusalem was in the war zone; therefore there could be no joint Anglo-French civilian administration. Only British military authorities could rule Palestine.[63]

Allenby's refusal to allow France to share in the administration of Palestine, in violation of the Sykes-Picot agreement, aroused French fears. Pichon was convinced, correctly so as events would reveal, that Lloyd George wanted "the annexation" of Palestine.[64] Pichon and Picot urged Premier Clemenceau to send at least one division to Palestine in order to protect France's political position in the Middle East. It was argued that without the presence of large-scale French reinforcements, England with 100,000 troops in the Middle East, would not abide by the Sykes-Picot agreement.[65] In March, 1918, Clemen-

---

[55] Picot to Pichon, Mar. 5, 1918, *ibid.*, vol. 884, fol. 129. See also Picot's views in Defrance to Pichon, Mar. 18, 1918, *ibid.*, fol. 162.

[56] Pichon to Picot, Mar. 19, 1918, *ibid.*, vol. 885, fol. 112.

[57] Chef au service d'informations de la Marine française dans le Levant to Georges Leygues, minister of the navy, Jan. 12, 1918, Archives Marine, carton Ea 200, dossier: 1918. See also Major Edouard Cousse, chief of the French military mission in Egypt, to Clemenceau, Mar. 1, 1918, AAE, série: Levant, 1918–1929, Arabie-Hedjaz, vol. 1.

[58] P. Cambon to Briand, Oct. 5, 1916, AAE, série: Guerre 1914–1918, vol. 874, fols. 121–123; Grey to Briand, Oct. 5, 1916, *ibid.*, fol. 124.

[59] Briand to P. Cambon, Oct. 9, 1916, *ibid.*, fol. 127.

[60] Briand to P. Cambon, Oct. 10, 11, 1916, *ibid.*, fols. 131, 133.

[61] Doynel de Saint-Quentin to Roques, Dec. 1, 1916, *ibid.*, vol. 875, fol. 2.

[62] Memo by Margerie, "Note pour M. le Président du Conseil," Dec. 14, 1916, *ibid.*, fol. 42; London Conference, Dec. 28, 1916, *ibid.*, fol. 73.

[63] Balfour to Pichon, Dec. 21, 1917, *ibid.*, vol. 881, fol. 103; Picot to Pichon, Jan. 26, 1918, *ibid.*, vol. 882, fols. 223–224; Allenby-Picot conversation of Dec. 4, 1917, in Briand to Roques, Dec. 12, 1917, Archives Marine, carton Ea 200, dossier: 1917.

[64] Pichon to P. Cambon, Dec. 25, 1917, AAE, série: Guerre 1914–1918, vol. 881, fol. 130.

[65] Pichon to Clemenceau, Dec. 12, 1917, *ibid.*, vol. 880, fol. 190; Pichon to Clemenceau, Jan. 15, 1918, *ibid.*, vol. 882, fols. 68–71; Picot to Pichon, Dec. 13, 1917, *ibid.*, vol. 880, fol. 197; Picot to Pichon, Jan. 20, 1918, *ibid.*, vol. 882, fols. 123–124. Clemenceau became prime minister in November, 1917.

ceau could send only a few troops to Palestine, increasing to 8,000 troops the French Detachment of Palestine.[66]

In September, 1918, Allenby's army crossed the Palestinian border into Syria. France immediately asked England to put the Sykes-Picot agreement into effect. Specifically, France requested that Picot be appointed high commissioner of Syria. As high commissioner Picot would have been the ruler of zone "A" of the Sykes-Picot agreement.[67] Arthur Balfour, Britain's foreign secretary, replied that he had never heard of the Sykes-Picot agreement. Balfour summoned Mark Sykes for an explanation of the agreement. Sykes told Balfour and Paul Cambon that the agreement was simply a project prepared by Picot that had been submitted to the committee of eastern affairs and "as such it could not be accepted without fundamental changes." Sykes also made some other disquieting statements. There could be no French high commissioner to Syria because it would undermine Allenby's authority. An Arab government would be established in Damascus, and France and Britain should issue a joint declaration that would "reassure" the Syrians as to French intentions.[68]

In the following days British intent became clearer. On September 26 Balfour told Pichon that Hussein should be formally recognized as a member of the Allied camp. France quickly agreed. The Hejaz would be sitting next to the United States, Great Britain, and France at the forthcoming peace conference.[69] On the same day Sykes and Picot met in London in an attempt to agree on a joint declaration to the Arabs. Picot said that France would "protect" Syria, develop its natural resources, administer equal justice to all groups, and bring an end to the religious and tribal divisions agonizing the country. Sykes rejected Picot's proposals. He claimed that Picot was advocating a French protectorate over zone "A." Picot thought that the 1916 agreements had given France a protectorate over Syria. Sykes retorted that the agreements had stipulated that England and France were the "co-guarantors" of an independent Syria.[70]

On September 27, as the British army advanced towards Damascus, Allenby told the French military attaché that "your cavalry is advancing with ours towards Damascus."[71] Four days later Allenby stopped the Allied advance and permitted Feisal's army to take Damascus. "Our permitting the occupation of Damascus by the Shereefians," observed General Clayton, "has allayed some of the [Arab] suspicion of the French intentions."[72] It did more than that. The delivery of Damascus to Feisal "created the myth of an Arab Revolt, advancing in triumph and crowning its progress with the capture of a great city, only to be cheated of victory by underhanded intrigues and sordid ambitions."[73]

On September 30 and October 22 England and France agreed to an arrangement for the military administration of Syria, Palestine, and Lebanon. Britain was to administer Palestine, France was to control the coastal area north of Palestine to Cilicia, and the Arabs were to administer Syria. Much to France's chagrin, eastern Lebanon was excluded from the French zone. Allenby arranged to have eastern Lebanon, which had been part of the French blue zone in the Sykes-Picot agreement, placed under Feisal's control.[74] France was disturbed by other aspects of the arrangement. Although France and England had agreed that Allenby would possess supreme authority, the French representative was to have been Allenby's principal political adviser. The French representative, ostensibly possessing a great deal of power, was to have been the only intermediary between Allenby and the Arab government. The French representative was to have supplied all the advisers to Feisal's Syrian government and was to have controlled the civil administration in the French zone.[75] Within a few weeks, however, Allenby had succeeded in undermining the agreement. The French could approach Feisal only through Allenby. Feisal's government was allowed complete freedom, whereas the French officials could not travel without Allenby's permission.[76] Furthermore, Allenby would not permit France to reinforce her coastal area. The general, motivated by political considerations, believed that the arrival of additional French troops would place France in a better position to rule Lebanon and Cilicia permanently.[77]

---

[66] Clemenceau to Pichon, Mar. 2, 1918, *ibid.*, vol. 884, fol. 101.

[67] Pichon to P. Cambon, Sept. 21, 1918, AAE, série: Levant, 1918–1929, Syrie-Liban-Cilicie (hereafter cited as Levant S-L-C), vol. 2, fol. 18.

[68] P. Cambon to Pichon, Sept. 28, 1918, *ibid.*, fols. 44–45.

[69] Balfour to Pichon, Sept. 26, 1918, AAE, série: Levant, 1918–1929, Arabie-Hedjaz, vol. 2, fol. 13.

[70] Sykes-Picot meeting, London, Sept. 26, 1918, AAE, série: Levant S-L-C, vol. 2, fol. 55.

[71] Captain Auguste-Jean-Robert Coulondre, interim high commissioner to Palestine and Syria, to Pichon, Sept. 27, 1918, *ibid.*, fol. 65.

[72] Clayton to the War Office, Oct. 8, 1918, Cab. 27/34, EC 1855.

[73] Kedourie, 1956: p. 122.

[74] Guichard, "Les Forces navales françaises en Syrie," n.d.: p. 748.

[75] P. Cambon to Pichon, Sept. 30, 1918, AAE, série: Levant S-L-C, vol. 2, fols. 84–86; Picot was the French representative. His title was French high commissioner to Palestine and Syria. However, he had no power in either region. England controlled Palestine and Feisal controlled Syria. More correctly, Picot's title should have been high commissioner to Lebanon.

[76] Quai d'Orsay memo, Nov. 30, 1918, *ibid.*, vol. 5, fol. 81.

[77] Allenby to War Office, Feb. 2, 1919, F.O. 371/4178, 2117/20447.

And the British blitz continued. On October 8 Balfour notified France that the defeat of Russia and the entry of the United States into the war meant that the 1916 Sykes-Picot agreement would have to be greatly changed.[78] A few days later France received a clearer idea of the type of changes England had in mind. Sykes told Picot that the best way "to reassure Feisal concerning French intentions" would be for France to give Feisal a portion of the French-occupied blue zone so that Syria would have an outlet on the Mediterranean.[79]

Obviously the British had decided that Feisal, not France, should rule Syria. This position had been supported, to some degree, in 1916 and 1917 by some British officials.[80] But it was only in 1918 when Allenby was advancing into Syria and the French had only a token force in the Middle East that the British government decided "to cancel the Sykes-Picot agreement, especially those clauses which confer rights upon France in area A and in the Syrian portion of the Blue zone (eastern Lebanon)." France could have the coastal areas of Lebanon and Alexandretta, but nothing else.[81] Why would England support Feisal at France's expense? The Foreign Office, which readily conceded that the Arabs had given "little military help" to Allenby's campaign, considered France a threat to British economic and imperial interests:

If we support the Arab movement we shall destroy Turkey with much less risk of arousing against us the permanent antagonism of Islam; and we shall knit up our Empire by establishing a link between Egypt and India, without being compelled to take France into partnership, and placing her in a position to break our newly-won territorial continuity. On the other hand, if we allow the Arab movement to fail, and Syria to pass from Turkish to French domination, . . . we shall place ourselves and France in a position in which our traditional rivalry in the East, which has been removed only with great difficulty, will be bound to arise again in an aggravated form.[82]

England utilized two techniques to advance her imperial interests. First, London championed Arab self-determination. This was intended to appeal to American President Woodrow Wilson. England expected Wilson to break the Sykes-Picot agreement at the forthcoming peace conference. Britain's interpretation of Arab self-determination was surprisingly restricted: basically it meant the absence of France from the Moslem Middle East. Once France had been removed, Great Britain expected to control the postwar Middle East, including Syria. General G. M. Macdonogh, British chief of military operations, noted:

There is a great difference in Arab sentiment regarding Syria and Mesopotamia. The Arabs are determined that in the former a purely Arab administration is to be established, and that they will not tolerate any foreign advisers or employees other than salaried servants of the Arab state. In Mesopotamia, however, they recognize the British right of conquest, and would acquiesce in a British protectorate. . . . At the same time the Syrian State should be united by close ties with Great Britain. Feisal is about to raise a force of 8,500 gendarmes . . . and a standing army of two brigades. . . . It is essential that these forces should be equipped by the British, as all Shereefian troops have hitherto been, and not by the French, and Feisal should be granted by Great Britain such financial assistance as he may need.
It must be remembered that it will be possible to raise an army of some 300,000 men in Syria. If the Government of that country is friendly to Great Britain it will be necessary to retain a far smaller British garrison in Egypt than if the Syrian administration is under French influence, and consequently a lesser drain will be imposed on the resources of the Empire.[83]

Lord Cecil, undersecretary of state for foreign affairs, also made a distinction between self-rule for the Arabs in Syria and those in Mesopotamia. He told the Eastern Committee in November, 1918, that in Mesopotamia

we ought to have a British-controlled Government, and I do not think there is any question at all that it ought to be in form an Arab Government. I go a little further than that, and aim ultimately at, if possible, setting up an Arab Government, if we can create one, in a generation or so. The doubt is as to the man. So far as that is concerned, personally I do not see anybody better than Abdullah. . . . Abdullah, from all I have heard of him, would do tolerably well if we have the right man to control him. He is . . . thought to be the cleverest of the Sherif's sons. He is a sensualist, idle, and very lazy.[84]

---

[78] Balfour to Pichon, Oct. 8, 1918, AAE, série: Levant S-L-C, vol. 2, fol. 184.

[79] Quai d'Orsay memo, "Note pour le ministre," Oct. 15, 1918, ibid., vol. 3, fol. 28.

[80] For example, see memo by Harold Nicolson, minor official in the Foreign Office, July 13, 1917, F.O. 371/3044, 1173/153075; Wingate to Balfour, June 11, 1917, F.O. 882/3, fol. 36.

[81] Recommendations of the Eastern Committee meeting held in early January, 1919, contained in memo by Sir Earle Richards, Jan., 1919, Lord Curzon Papers, F 112/266. See also General G. M. Macdonogh, British chief of military operations, "Note on Policy in the Middle East," submitted to the War Cabinet, Oct. 28, 1918, Cab. 27/35, EC 2133; Eastern Committee meeting, Nov. 27, 1918, F.O. 371/4148, 144/13298; memo by Arthur Nicolson, "Settlement of Turkey and Arabian Peninsula," Nov. 30, 1918, F.O. 371/3385, 747/199474.

[82] Arnold Toynbee, "Memorandum on French and Arab Claims . . . to British Interests," Dec. 19, 1918, F.O. 371/3385, 747/191229. Toynbee worked in the Intelligence division of the Foreign Office. The report is quoted in Kedourie, 1976: p. 213.

[83] General G. M. Macdonogh, "Note on Policy in the Middle East," Oct. 28, 1918, Cab. 27/35, EC 2133, p. 2.

[84] Eastern Committee meeting, Nov. 27, 1918, F.O. 371/4148, 144/13298, p. 9. When he heard Cecil's description of Abdullah, Lord Curzon appropriately piped up: "Where has Abdullah been all this while?" ibid. At this time Lord Curzon was lord president.

A second method employed by England to justify the repudiation of certain clauses in the Sykes-Picot agreement was to reinterpret McMahon's October 24, 1915, letter to Hussein. Foreign Secretary Balfour claimed in February, 1918, that McMahon's letter had promised an independent state to the Arabs. The only qualifications that Balfour noticed in the letter were that Mersina and Alexandretta were not to be part of the Arab state and that Hussein had been warned that English interests in Mesopotamia "would necessitate special measures of administrative control."[85] Balfour had conveniently overlooked the key qualifying clause in the letter: England could not "act without detriment to her ally, France." Balfour may have overlooked something else: a Foreign Office study of the McMahon-Hussein correspondence. This early 1918 report stated that British "commitments to King Hussein are not embodied in any agreement or treaty signed, or even acknowledged by both parties." The detailed report also stated that Britain had "committed themselves to no special position towards King Hussein which is incompatible with their agreements with France."[86] Nevertheless, the British government, led by Balfour, now believed that the McMahon letter had involved Great Britain in a contractual agreement wherein Syria had been promised to the Sherifians.

France did not immediately grasp the intensity or the depth of Britain's Middle Eastern plans. Pichon responded to the late 1918 British offensive by appealing to the familiar: the Sykes-Picot agreement was an honest bargain based "on the recognition of the respective aspirations of the two countries in areas in which they have always had connections, interests, and rights."[87] The British response was brutal. On November 27 Balfour warned Clemenceau that, if the Sykes-Picot agreement remained unchanged, England at the forthcoming Paris peace conference would not support French policies in Western Europe.[88] The British warning outraged the French. The French bitterly complained that, since British troops dominated the entire Middle East and "their puppet Feisal" controlled Syria, the English were going to renege on the Sykes-Picot agreement just as they were preparing to do with the St. Jean de Maurienne pact. There was one way to stop the British steamroller: "Have the necessary batallions ready for the occupation of Syria. On that day let us flatly ask Great Britain to withdraw her troops."[89]

The British ambassador to France, Lord Derby, could not understand the reason for France's anger. He reassured Balfour:

The loyalty of the British cabinet has been perfect. It has been careful to repeat that the interests of France in the East must not suffer from the excessive concentration of French troops on the Western Front. It is nevertheless true that independently of London, the *de facto* situation in Syria works against France, and that in the East, more than anywhere else, "les absents ont souvent tort," and that one cannot be too clear or precise in the manner.[90]

Lord Derby was correct. England had the upper hand. France had little choice. France would need British support at the peace conference.[91] Consequently on December 2, 1918, Clemenceau traveled to London and met with Lloyd George. In a verbal understanding without witnesses and with no written record Clemenceau agreed to modify the Sykes-Picot agreement. The oil-producing area of Mosul, which in 1916 had been placed in the French zone, would be transferred to the British sphere. Palestine, which in 1916 had been reserved for some form of international control, would also be transferred to the British sphere. In return, the British prime minister tentatively agreed to support French claims to Syria and Cilicia.[92]

French insistence on maintaining the Sykes-Picot agreement had led to a painful collision with England. France's policy towards Feisal was fruitless as well. Picot, French high commissioner at Beirut, wondered in mid-November, 1918, which policy France should adopt towards Feisal. Should France offer Feisal a shadowy kingship of Lebanon and Syria in return for greater French control of the two countries? Should France allow him a good deal of political liberty in Syria in return for his recognition of a French-controlled Lebanon? Should France encourage dissident groups within Syria in hopes of overthrowing him? Or did the French have a choice? The Lebanese Catholics would reject a Sherifian kingship and England could easily prevent the overthrow of Feisal.[93]

Although answers to Picot's questions were not immediately forthcoming, the Quai d'Orsay on the

---

[85] Balfour, "Synopsis of Our Obligations to Our Allies and Others," submitted to the War Cabinet, Feb. 6, 1918, Cab. 1/26.

[86] Foreign Office memo, "Memorandum on British Commitments to King Hussein," Feb. (?), 1918, Cab. 27/36, EC 2201.

[87] Pichon to P. Cambon, Oct. 21, 1918, AAE, série: Levant S-L-C, vol. 3, fol. 110.

[88] Balfour to Pichon, Nov. 26, 1918, *ibid.*, vol. 5, fol. 63.

[89] Quai d'Orsay memo, Nov. 30, 1918, *ibid.*, fols. 81–82.

[90] Lord Derby to Balfour, Dec. 12, 1918, F.O. 371/3386, 747/204960.

[91] Pichon to Balfour, Nov. 30, 1918, AAE, série: Levant S-L-C, vol. 5, fol. 83.

[92] David Lloyd George, *Memoirs of the Peace Conference* (2 v., New Haven, 1939) **2**: p. 673; Quai d'Orsay memo, "Note au sujet d'une Entente franco-anglaise sur la question de Syrie," Feb. 9, 1919, AAE, série: Levant S-L-C, vol. 9, fols. 151, 153, 156.

[93] Picot to Pichon, Nov. 16, 1918, AMG, 7N 2145, dossier 7.

eve of the Paris peace conference was attempting to shape a coherent Middle Eastern policy. First, Pichon decided that France could no longer ignore Feisal. The Sherifian would be coming to the peace conference and it seemed necessary for France to negotiate with him. However, the French expected to negotiate with him as if he were a tribal chieftain, not the leader of Syria. France would attempt to seek two prerequisites before agreeing to negotiate with Feisal. French troops must replace all English troops in Syria, and France, not England, must subsidize the Syrian ruler.[94] If these changes were implemented, the Quai d'Orsay wistfully believed that an intimidated Feisal would turn away from England and "seek support from the French."[95]

Secondly, the Quai d'Orsay considered the threat posed by Arab nationalism and the Wilsonian ideals of self-determination for the native population. France, it was maintained, need not repudiate the legitimate aspirations of the Arabs. But self-determination should not be limited to the Sunni and Shiite Moslems. The other ethnic and religious groups, such as Christians, Druzes, and Alawites, should also be given some political autonomy. France's basic role would be that of a "disinterested" arbiter keeping the peace among the traditionally hostile groups. The humanitarian justification for France's presence in the Middle East was also intended to serve a practical function: to keep England out of Syria. Britain already controlled Mecca, Cairo, and Baghdad. English domination of Damascus would have given Britain unprecedented power in the Moslem world and would, it was feared, have created an "inadmissible danger" for France's position in North Africa.[96]

This emphasis upon the autonomy of the various religious and ethnic communities explains why France joined England in a famous joint declaration of intent. The two countries publicly announced on November 7, 1918, that they sought "the complete and definite emancipation of the peoples so long oppressed by the Turks and the establishment of national governments and administrations deriving their authority from the initiative and free choice of the indigenous populations." France and England intended to assist "the establishment of indigenous Governments and administrations in Syria and Mesopotamia." The British and Arabs thought that this declaration meant that France had agreed to the creation of an independent Syrian state. The French, however, meant that all indigenous groups within Syria should be given the right to establish governments. Pichon explained that "the Anglo-French declaration refers particularly to the peoples of the Syrian and Arab areas ... who are requesting assurance that their autonomy will be fully safeguarded under French ... protection."[97]

A third response to Feisal involved a more fundamental change in France's Middle Eastern policy. In late 1918 the Quai d'Orsay realized that Feisal had a good deal of popular Arab support and that much of that recent support stemmed from France's wartime Zionist policies. To undercut some of this popularity France decided to change her Zionist policies.

France's first wartime contact with Zionism came from the American Jewish community. In October, 1914, American Zionists petitioned the French embassy in Washington, asking that once the war were ended, Palestine be reserved for a Jewish Homeland.[98] The idea of creating a Jewish state quickly gave way to more immediate Zionist concerns. Prominent American Zionists besieged the French government with demands that wartime czarist Russia stop mistreating her Jewish population.[99]

As a means to counter the effects of Russian anti-Semitism, France sent two French Jews to tour neutralist America. Naoum Slousch and Victor Basch, in late 1915 and early 1916, explained to the American Jewish community that Germany was much more anti-Semitic than the Allied countries. The two propagandists dutifully reported to the French government that two prerequisites must be met if the Allies hoped to win American Jewish support. Russian persecution of Jews must stop, and the Allies must guarantee that Palestine be reserved as a Jewish

---

[94] Quai d'Orsay memo, "Note pour le ministre," Nov. 15, 1918, AAE, série: Levant S-L-C, vol. 4, fol. 152.

[95] Pichon, "Note pour Monsieur le Président du Conseil," Jan. 9, 1919, AMG, 6N 197, dossier: Syrie, Cilicie, Beyrouth.

[96] Quai d'Orsay memo, "Affaires d'Orient: révisions éventuelles des accords de 1916," Nov. 24, 1918, AAE, série: Levant S-L-C, vol. 5, fols. 21–22.

[97] Pichon to Barrère, Nov. 2, 1918, ibid., vol. 4, fol. 12. London and Paris spent almost a month working on the wording of the declaration. The British sought to include in the declaration a statement that the two countries would not annex any territories in the Middle East unless invited to do so by the native population. Since British troops controlled the area, France feared that such an invitation would be very likely. See Quai d'Orsay memo, Oct. 15, 1918, ibid., vol. 3, fols. 30–31; P. Cambon to Pichon, Oct. 17, 26, 1915, ibid., fols. 45, 201; Quai d'Orsay memo, "Observations," Oct. 25, 1918, ibid., fol. 188.

[98] Jean Jusserand, French ambassador to the United States, to Delcassé, Oct. 6, 1914, AAE, série: Guerre 1914–1918, vol. 1197, fol. 1.

[99] Jusserand to Delcassé, Nov. 20, 1914, Feb. 12, Mar. 10, 18, 1915, ibid., fols. 3, 25, 29, 30. France, sensitive to any requests coming from neutralist America, asked its ambassador in Petrograd to intervene on behalf of the Russian Jews. Paléologue reported that the "slightest appearance of foreign interference would be fatal to the Jewish cause because it would immediately provoke an upsurgence of religious and national consciousness throughout Russia" (Paléologue to Delcassé, July 18, 1915, ibid., fol. 43).

state.[100] Briand promptly told the American Zionists in early 1916 that "the extension and liberty of Jewish colonies in Palestine [would] not be forgotten by France and England."[101] The American Zionists, however, considered Briand's statement inadequate. They wanted a Jewish state.[102] France was not yet prepared to go that far.

A year later, however, Zionism took on a new significance for the Allies. As Russia suffered from political upheaval and military collapse, France and England sought means to help their ally. One method to increase Jewish enthusiasm for the provisional government and the Russian war effort would be to demonstrate that a Jewish state in Palestine was closely tied to an Allied triumph.[103] France also feared the possibility that Germany would promise Palestine to the Zionists. Such a move, France thought, might win support for Germany within the American Jewish community. The impact upon the United States could be decisive. "If the Jewish financial community of New York should side with the Germans, all that could weigh heavily on the decisions taken by Mr. Wilson."[104]

In March, 1917, Nahum Sokolow, executive chairman of the Zionist International Committee, arrived in Paris. Sokolow explained the Zionist program to the Ribot government: recognition of Palestine as a "national country" for the Jews, an Allied protectorate for Palestine, Jewish self-determination and complete autonomy for domestic affairs in Palestine, a charter company to promote colonization to Palestine, and no restrictions on Jewish immigration to Palestine. Jules Cambon, secretary-general of the Quai d'Orsay, told Sokolow that "the French government could not look unfavorably upon the claims tending to the liberation of an oppressed race."[105] Two months later, on June 4, Cambon was more explicit. He wrote Sokolow:

> You were good enough to present the project to which you are devoting your efforts, which has for its object the development of Jewish colonization in Palestine. You consider that, circumstances permitting, and the independence of the Holy Places being safeguarded on the other hand, it would be a deed of justice and of reparation to assist, by the protection of the Allied Powers, in the renaissance of the Jewish nationality in that Land from which the people of *Israel* were exiled so many centuries ago.
>
> The French Government, which entered this present war to defend a people wrongfully attacked, . . . can but feel sympathy for your cause, the triumph of which is bound up with that of the Allies.

I am happy to give you herewith such assurance.[106]

France, which recognized Jewish nationality and its historical right to Palestine, had become the first European country to acknowledge officially the legitimacy of the Zionist program.

In November, 1917, Great Britain issued the Balfour Declaration, promising the Jews a "national home" in Palestine. Although the Balfour and Cambon declarations carry the same message, France initially refused to endorse the Balfour Declaration. The Zionists were no longer needed now that the United States was committed to the Entente and Russia lay prostrate and helpless. Furthermore, the highly assimilated French Jews were anti-Zionist and Pichon now found it convenient to satisfy French Jewry. But the most important reason for French hesitancy was the belief that Zionism was a liability to France's postwar Middle Eastern policies.[107] Picot, who supported Zionist aspirations in the spring of 1917,[108] told Pichon a few weeks following the publication of the Balfour Declaration that the Moslems would never accept the Jews in Palestine. France would alienate the Arabs if she supported the Balfour Declaration. It would be better, advised Picot, to have Arab hostility directed against Great Britain rather than against France.[109]

The view from the United States was altogether different. André Tardieu, French high commissioner to the United States, urged Pichon in January, 1918, to endorse the Balfour Declaration. Tardieu maintained that French domestic politics should not influence the government's attitude toward Zionism; simply because French Jews were hostile to Zionism did not mean that the French government should pursue a policy contrary to that of England and the United States. Tardieu also dismissed the argument that endorsement of the Balfour Declaration would lead to Arab hostility. England had millions of Moslem subjects yet she had issued the Balfour Declaration. Perhaps the most persuasive argument put forth by Tardieu was to point out that several of President Wilson's advisers were Zionists. These Jewish advisers would have a good deal of influence at the peace conference. If France failed to support the Zionists, Tardieu asked, would Wilson's advisers fail to support France's postwar claims to Alsace-Lorraine.[110]

---

[100] Jusserand to Briand, Dec. 17, 1915, *ibid.*, fol. 115.
[101] Briand to Jusserand, Feb. 12, 1916, *ibid.*, fol. 140.
[102] Memo by Slousch, Apr. 10, 1916, *ibid.*, vol. 1198, fol. 2.
[103] Ribot to Picot, Apr. 2, 1917, *ibid.*, vol. 876, fol. 139; Ribot to Jusserand, Aug. 30, 1917, *ibid.*, vol. 1199, fol. 137.
[104] Memo by Jules Cambon, secretary-general of the Quai d'Orsay, Mar. 11, 1917, *ibid.*, vol. 1198, fol. 117.
[105] Picot to Ribot, May 5, 1917, *ibid.*, vol. 1199, fols. 3–4.

[106] J. Cambon to Sokolow, June 4, 1917, quoted in Nahum Sokolow, *History of Zionism, 1600–1918* (2 v. in 1, New York, 1969) **2**: p. 53.
[107] Pichon to André Tardieu, French high commissioner to the United States, Jan. 26, 1918, AAE, série: Guerre 1914–1918, vol. 1200, fol. 205.
[108] Picot to Ribot, May 5, 1917, *ibid.*, vol. 1199, fol. 4.
[109] Picot to Pichon, Nov. 27, Dec. 6, 1917, *ibid.*, fols. 61–62, 79. Picot's views were shared by Defrance (Defrance to Pichon, Nov. 27, 1917, *ibid.*, fol. 59).
[110] Tardieu to Clemenceau, Jan. 17, 1918, *ibid.*, vol. 1200,

Tardieu's arguments were effective. On February 9 Pichon told Sokolow that England and France had agreed on the question of "a Jewish settlement in Palestine."[111] Sokolow requested further clarification. Jewish settlements had been in Palestine for centuries. Pichon announced a few days later that France agreed that the Palestinian Jews would be "given administrative autonomy within the framework of an international state."[112] Several months later in October, Pichon strongly suggested that the Jews would enjoy political as well as administrative rights:

Nothing therefore stands in the way of the people of Palestine aspiring to supervised autonomy. I shall even go further; a promise of this sort was implicitly made to the Zionists when France and Great Britain agreed to the formation of a Jewish Home in Palestine.[113]

However, by January, 1919, French support of Zionism had evaporated. Frequent clashes between Palestinian Jews and Arabs in late 1918 increased Arab nationalism. Feisal's prestige thrived on the Arabs' anti-Zionism. Palestinian Arabs optimistically considered Feisal as the only Arab leader "capable of resisting the Jewish flood" into Palestine.[114] France feared the increase of Arab nationalism. Consequently, Pichon criticized the Zionists as troublemakers whose presence in Palestine only served "to spread intrigues undertaken by some Pan-Arab leaders."[115]

In addition, Clemenceau's December, 1918, decision to give Palestine to England meant that there was no advantage for France, wholly interested in ruling millions of Moslems and Christians in Lebanon and Syria, to support or even defend the Zionists in Palestine. Thus France not only repudiated the idea of an independent Jewish state in Palestine, but for the first time also rejected any kind of "sovereign Jewish organism" in the Middle East.[116] Pichon in tortured fashion would only agree to something called a "moral and intellectual Jewish homeland in Palestine," that is, one devoid of any political, administrative, or economic autonomy—a non-state.[117]

Although anti-Zionist, French policy on the eve of the peace conference was not pro-Arab. The core of France's Middle Eastern policy was a slightly modified version of the Sykes-Picot agreement. Pichon also had a formula, one based on self-determination, which he expected could achieve the goals of the Sykes-Picot agreement. Whether this formula would permit France to control Syria and Lebanon without apparently undermining Wilsonian ideals and British strategic and economic interests remained to be seen.

3. FRENCH FAILURE IN PARIS

The Paris peace conference convened in mid-January, 1919. On January 30 the Allies agreed to a British-sponsored proposal that the former Turkish territories should receive administrative and political advice and assistance from a mandatory power until these states were considered economically and politically mature enough to stand alone. However, as a concession to Wilsonian principles, the native population would receive the right to select the mandatory power. The mandatory power would be responsible to the League of Nations for its actions.

France immediately seized advantage of this latest development. Paris promptly grafted the Sykes-Picot agreement to Wilsonian ideals. Pichon proposed to the British on February 6 that the zone of French influence ("A") and the zone of direct sovereignty (blue) of the Sykes-Picot agreement be abolished. He wanted Cilicia, Lebanon, and Syria to be merged and given to France as a League mandate. Pichon emphasized that France's record of tutelage and protection in the Middle East was unsurpassed. For several centuries France had been building hospitals, orphanages, and schools for both Christians and Moslems. Pichon pleaded:

These countries need her assistance more than ever because if they are left to their own devices without any preparation for self-government and because of their diversity of race and religion, they are liable to disorders which only the authority of an impartial and respected arbiter can allay.

France, as a sop to Arab nationalism, was prepared to reach an accommodation with Feisal. He could be the Emir of Damascus with France supplying his advisers and controlling his domestic and foreign policies.[1]

Why did France so readily accept the concept of a mandate? The mandate system was a means to satisfy the Allies' territorial ambitions without incurring the taint of annexation and the wrath of Presi-

---

fols. 85–88; Tardieu to Pichon, Jan. 30, 1918, *ibid.*, fols. 111–112.

[111] Quai d'Orsay memo, Feb. 9, 1918, *ibid.*, fol. 144.
[112] Pichon to Tardieu, Feb. 14, 1918, *ibid.*, fol. 171.
[113] Pichon to P. Cambon, Oct. 10, 1918, AAE, série: Levant, 1918–1929, Palestine, vol. 11, fol. 33. The Balfour Declaration speaks of political rights for the Jews in Palestine.
[114] Paul-Marie Durieux, delegate of French high commissioner in Palestine, to Picot, Dec. 4, 1918, *ibid.*, fols. 250–251. See also Durieux to Picot, Nov. 5, 16, Dec. 13, 1918, *ibid.*, fols. 100, 197–198, 208.
[115] Pichon to P. Cambon, Jan. 15, 1919, *ibid.*, vol. 12, fols. 52–53.
[116] *Ibid.*, fol. 53.
[117] Pichon to Defrance, Jan. 12, 1919, *ibid.*, fol. 46. Pichon cautioned England "to abstain from all acts or declarations which would give the Jews any unattainable hopes" (Pichon to P. Cambon, Jan. 15, 1919, *ibid.*, fol. 53).

[1] Pichon to Balfour, Feb. 6, 1919, AAE, série: Levant S-L-C, vol. 9, fols. 87–91.

dent Woodrow Wilson.² The *Correspondance d'Orient,* a strident defender of French imperialism, believed that the mandate system would allow France to fulfill her "civilizing mission" while protecting her vital self interests. Millions of Moslems with French and British assistance "must gradually be led towards Western Civilization." Would that not be "a plan which corresponds exactly to the necessities of [French and British] foreign and colonial policies?"³

At the same time the concept of a mandate was seen as only a slight variation of contemporary French colonial doctrine. The theory of the association, the ideological foundation of French imperial rule, was based on the idea that France should tutor the colonial societies and help them to evolve according to their own potentialities. Association argued, at least in theory, for a mutually advantageous cooperation between a superior, France, and an inferior, the colony. The mandate system, on the other hand, was predicated on a relationship between equals. Nevertheless, the mandate system could serve France's purpose just as well as association had done. A paternalistic France could guide, educate, and protect Syria and Lebanon until a native elite could be trained.⁴

Although Georges Clemenceau and Stéphen Pichon favored a French mandate, not all French officials were as sanguine about its benefits. Paul Cambon predicted a "good deal of embarrassment" if France assumed the mandate. Syria, Lebanon, and Cilicia were split into a myriad of races, religions, and clans. Foreign powers, he maintained, would soon support the grievances of some of these groups. As a means to champion their "clients," foreign powers would use the forum of the League of Nations to criticize France.⁵

A minority within the Quai d'Orsay argued that it was not in France's interests to assume control of Syria and Cilicia. France had popular support only from the Lebanese Catholics; consequently, France should have close political ties only with Lebanon. Cilicia and to a lesser extent Syria offered exceptional economic opportunities. But France could never fully develop these areas. Instead, France would have to pour out huge sums of money to support an occupation army, if only to maintain a semblance of law and order among the Arabs, Kurds, Turks, and Armenians. Likewise, large amounts of French capital would be needed for railway construction, reopening of the mines, oil exploration in the Mosul area, large-scale agricultural development, and harbor and port improvements after years of war and neglect. French manpower, capital, and energy were needed elsewhere. A war-devastated France should be concerned in the first place with her domestic recovery. Neither did France's second priority reside in the Middle East. "Before any other distant undertaking it is important for France to consolidate her political and economic settlement in North Africa."⁶

The economic burden of a French military occupation in Syria was appreciated by others within Pichon's entourage. But this was considered to be a small price to pay. France's North African empire was at stake:

Damascus is a Moslem center which is very hostile to France, to tell the truth the most hostile in all Islam. It is there where the fanatic Arabs of North Africa go who want to elude our control. It is there where all the plots against our authority in the Moslem countries are hatched, and it is there where the agitators who come and preach rebellion in our Moslem possessions start out. It is certainly this state of things . . . which makes it desirable that Damascus be placed under our control.⁷

The survival of French influence, however, was the key issue for many at the Quai d'Orsay, including Pichon. English policies during the preceding six months had confirmed France's worst fears: Britain hoped to increase her empire and influence by attempting to drive France out of the Middle East. Feisal was to be the instrument for this policy. The British had established him in Damascus, allowed him to be the *de facto* ruler of Syria, and continued to subsidize him. And it was London that had notified a startled France that Feisal would be brought to the peace conference to plead his case for an independent Syria. To break this British hold and to reassert French prestige, Pichon wanted French troops to replace the British garrisons in Cilicia, Syria, and eastern Lebanon.⁸

French claims to Syria were first presented to the Paris peace conference on February 13 by the chair-

---

² Pichon to Balfour, Feb. 6, 1919, *ibid.,* fol. 89; Quai d'Orsay memo, "Accord sur la Syrie-Cilicie," Mar. 17, 1919, *ibid.,* vol. 25, fol. 108.

³ Georges Samné, "La Collaboration franco-anglaise nécessaire," *Correspondance d'Orient,* no. 210 (Mar. 30, 1919): p. 251.

⁴ Albert Sarraut, *La Mise en valeur des colonies françaises* (Paris, 1923), chap. iii.

⁵ P. Cambon to Pichon, Mar. 3, 1919, AAE, série: Levant S-L-C, vol. 10, fol. 123.

⁶ Quai d'Orsay memo, "Note sur la Cilicie et le Kurdistan," Feb. 5, 1919, *ibid.,* vol. 9, fols. 100–102.

⁷ Quai d'Orsay memo, "Note sur la Syrie," Feb. 14, 1919, *ibid.,* vol. 10, fol. 46.

⁸ Pichon, "Note pour Monsieur le Président du Conseil," Jan. 9, 1919, AMG, 6N 197, dossier: Syrie, Cilicie, Beyrouth. See also Quai d'Orsay memo, "Note pour le général Belin," Jan., 1919, AAE, série: Levant S-L-C, vol. 9, fols. 18–19; Quai d'Orsay memo, "Note au sujet d'une entente franco-anglaise sur la question de Syrie," Feb. 9, 1919, *ibid.,* fols. 151–156. France's leading Middle Eastern officials favored a French mandate. See Coulondre, "Etude sur la question syrienne," Jan. 30, 1919, AAE, série: Papiers d'agents: Jean Goût, caisse 7; Picot to Pichon, Feb. 16, 1919, AAE, série: Levant S-L-C, vol. 9, fol. 263.

man of the Central Syrian Committee, Chekri Ganem. The Central Syrian Committee, with close ties to the Quai d'Orsay, claimed to represent those Syrians scattered throughout the world. Ganem argued that the Syrians were not prepared to govern themselves. Economic and political assistance would be needed. France, Ganem claimed, should be the country to "guide" Syria. France was qualified for this assignment because it had successfully ruled 25 million Moslems in North Africa and had strong ties with the Christian communities in the Middle East.[9]

On March 20 President Wilson, Pichon, Lloyd George, Allenby, and Clemenceau met for the first time to discuss the Syrian question. Pichon requested that France receive the mandate for Syria and Lebanon. He also believed that, with the good offices of Great Britain, France could reach an understanding with Feisal. The 1916 Sykes-Picot agreement served as the basis for the French claim. Lloyd George promptly pointed out that Pichon had misread the Sykes-Picot agreement. The agreement gave France direct control only in the blue zone; thus, France was entitled only to a Lebanese mandate. According to Lloyd George the Sykes-Picot agreement first and foremost stipulated that France would recognize an independent Arab state in zone "A." Lloyd George refused to permit France to have the Syrian mandate and insisted that Feisal be recognized as the ruler of an independent Syria. The British prime minister next asserted that, if France took Syria, it would be a violation of Britain's promises of independence to the Arabs. He insisted that McMahon's October 24, 1915, letter to Hussein had promised an independent Syria to the Arabs. Lloyd George had clearly dismissed the opinion of Robert Cecil, a member of the British peace conference delegation. Six weeks earlier Cecil, who wanted Feisal to control Syria, had written the prime minister that England was under no legal obligation to Feisal: "I do not say that if we do not give Damascus to Feisal we shall be guilty of an actual breach of faith, but we shall undoubtedly disappoint hopes which we have allowed—I think one must say encouraged, him to entertain." [10]

When Pichon complained that all promises to the Arabs were British ones and in no way involved France, Lloyd George bluntly reminded the French that it was England which had committed more than one million troops against the Turks. The Arabs had contributed to this campaign, therefore they deserved an independent Syria. Lloyd George then asked Allenby what would happen if France were to occupy Syria. Not unexpectedly, Allenby responded that the Arabs would resist the French occupation. Allenby added that a French incursion into Syria raised the possibility of setting off a large-scale Arab revolt throughout the Middle East, one involving the British in Palestine, Mesopotamia, and Egypt.

As the gap between England and France widened, on March 20 President Wilson intervened. Wilson noted that one of the parties to the 1916 agreement, Czarist Russia, no longer existed. Therefore, the original agreement was void. He maintained that the only way to settle the Syrian problem would be to send an Interallied Inquiry Commission there in order to ascertain the views of the population. Clemenceau said that he agreed with Wilsonian ideals of self-determination, but "something must be said for [France's] historical claims." Nevertheless, he accepted the proposal. Not to have done so would have been to reject one of the basic principles under which the peace conference operated. However, he insisted, much to England's discomfort, that the inquiry be extended to Palestine and Mesopotamia. If the Syrians were to be given an opportunity to determine their fate, Arabs elsewhere should be given the same opportunity.[11]

Rebuffed by England, France now turned to Feisal. Although the Syrian ruler had been in Paris for three months, there had been no serious discussions with the French. On February 6 Feisal had addressed the peace conference. He had asked for a unified, independent Arab state. He had also requested that the Arabs be allowed to select the mandatory power and that they be permitted to determine the extent of assistance to be received from the European power. Feisal's argument for Arab independence was based on the principles of self-determination as put forth in President Wilson's Fourteen Points. At no time in his presentation did Feisal make reference to McMahon's alleged promises to give Syria to the Sherifians.[12] Although Feisal "made a very great impression and is much the most dignified figure at the Conference,"[13] Pichon had not been impressed. He had dismissed all of Feisal's pleas for Syrian independence as a British ploy intended to deprive France of a place in the postwar Middle East.[14]

In late March, Colonel Lawrence, Feisal's adviser

---

[9] "Secretary's Notes . . . 13 February, 1919, at 3 P.M.," United States, Department of State, *Papers Relating to the Foreign Relations of the United States, 1919: The Paris Peace Conference* (13 v., Washington, D.C., 1942–1947; hereafter cited as USFR) **3**: pp. 1024–1038.

[10] Cecil to Lloyd George, Feb. 4, 1919, Lloyd George Papers, F/6/6/5.

[11] For the minutes of the March 20, 1919, meeting, see "Notes of a Conference . . . March 20, 1919," USFR **5**: pp. 1–14.

[12] "Secretary's Notes of a Conversation Held . . . 6 February 1919," *ibid*. **3**: pp. 889–894.

[13] Sir James Headlam-Morley, *A Memoir of the Paris Peace Conference, 1919* (London, 1972), pp. 30–31.

[14] Pichon to Picot, Feb. 13, 1919, AAE, série: Levant, 1918–1929, Arabie-Hedjaz, vol. 3, fol. 119; Pichon, "Note pour M. Goût," Feb. 6, 1919, *ibid*., fol. 106.

and confidant, informed the Quai d'Orsay that Feisal was prepared to accept a French mandate. France would supply Feisal's advisers and control Syria's foreign policy. In return, Feisal wanted Lebanon to be part of a "Greater Syria" and more vaguely, the Syrians should be given the right to choose their government and rulers.[15] France had something that Feisal and the Syrian nationalists wanted—Lebanon. Feisal feared that the Inquiry Commission would reveal that the Lebanese Christians did not want to live under Moslem control. Secondly, an understanding between the French and Feisal would abort the possibility of an Anglo-French agreement; the British were greatly concerned about the implications of an inquiry commission in Mesopotamia.[16]

Robert de Caix, technical adviser to the French delegation at the peace conference, successfully argued that France must accept Feisal's offer to negotiate an agreement. If Feisal needed France, France certainly needed Feisal. An agreement with Feisal was the only acceptable means by which France could gain a foothold in Syria. And an agreement was needed before the Inquiry Commission revealed that Moslems did not want French tutelage. Any kind of agreement, no matter how vague concerning the question of sovereignty, would be of value if it permitted French troops to enter Syria. Once established, France would rule the country. Not even the League of Nations, De Caix asserted, would curb French actions in Syria. England would not want Syrian nationalism to disrupt British control of Mesopotamia. And if the United States were to obtain the Armenian mandate, as some were proposing at the peace conference, the Americans would quickly learn to be "indulgent" of the other mandatory powers in the Middle East.[17]

France now set forth the basis of an agreement with Feisal. France was prepared to recognize the existence of a "Greater Syria," that is, a union of Syria and Lebanon. In return, Feisal would have to accept French economic and military advisers. He must recognize publicly France's historical contribution to the Middle East. Lastly, the new state, "Greater Syria," must be based on a federation of different, local, autonomous groups.[18] The creation of autonomous entities would prevent the Christians from panicking and, more importantly, perpetuate the deep religious and tribal divisions within Syrian society, thereby allowing France to control the country more easily. A badly splintered country, where differences were emphasized, would offer France the opportunity to arbitrate the many factional disputes. As long as France had to keep the peace among the various groups, she could justify her presence in Syria as a humanitarian necessity.[19]

On April 7 Lawrence, who wore an Arab headcloth at the conference when "he believed that it would strengthen the Arab position,"[20] submitted Feisal's offer. The Syrian proposal first reminded France of her very vulnerable position. British troops controlled the Middle East. Furthermore, the Sykes-Picot agreement stipulated that France could supply advisers to zone "A" but only if the Arabs asked for the advisers. Feisal had not yet asked for French assistance and he warned that he might never do so unless there were an agreement. Specifically, Feisal wanted France "to exchange her present great privileges on the coast [Lebanon] for lesser privileges extending equally over the coast and the interior [Syria]." What would these "lesser privileges" in a "Greater Syria" entail? France could have "economic and financial opportunities." Meanwhile Feisal would have satisfied the Arab nationalists who wanted a "Greater Syria."[21]

Paris immediately rejected the proposals. Feisal had not acknowledged French tutelage. Furthermore, France could not deliver Lebanon to Syria in return for the "possibility of developing some commercial enterprises."[22] Picot immediately visited Feisal and told him that it would be unwise to return to Syria without an agreement with France. Failure in Paris would strengthen the Syrian nationalists; consequently, the possibility of future agreement would be much more difficult to arrange. Feisal asked that "a qualified authority give me exact guarantees as to Syrian independence and . . . [I will] induce the population to accept French cooperation."[23]

On April 13 Clemenceau met Feisal and promised that France would recognize Syrian independence. However, he also insisted that French troops occupy Damascus. Feisal thought that there was a "contradiction" between the principle of independence and

---

[15] De Caix to Berthelot, Mar. 27, 1919, AAE, série: Levant S-L-C, vol. 11, fols. 131–132.

[16] P. Cambon to Pichon, Apr. 2, 1919, AAE, série: Levant, Arabie-Hedjaz, vol. 4, fol. 15.

[17] De Caix to Berthelot, Mar. 27, 1919, AAE, série: Levant S-L-C, vol. 11, fols. 133–134.

[18] P. Cambon to Pichon, Apr. 2, 1919, AAE, série: Levant, Arabie-Hedjaz, vol. 4, fol. 16.

[19] Quai d'Orsay memo, "But de la note Lawrence-Faysal," Apr. 10, 1919, ibid., fol. 34.

[20] John E. Mack, *A Prince of Our Disorder: The Life of T. E. Lawrence* (London, 1976), p. 264.

[21] Quai d'Orsay memo, "Note remise par le colonel Lawrence à M. Clemenceau," Apr. 7, 1919, AAE, série: Levant S-L-C, vol. 11, fols. 247–249.

[22] Quai d'Orsay memo, "But de la note Lawrence-Faysal," Apr. 10, 1919, AAE, série: Levant, Arabie-Hedjaz, vol. 4, fol. 34; anon., "Analyse de la note," Apr. 10(?), 1919, AAE, série: Levant S-L-C, vol. 11, fols. 254–256.

[23] Quai d'Orsay memo, "Note de M. Picot," Apr. 8, 1919, AAE, série: Levant S-L-C, vol. 11, fols. 250–251. See also Quai d'Orsay memo, "Note," Apr. 8, 1919, ibid., fol. 228.

a French military occupation.[24] Nevertheless, four days later Clemenceau submitted an agreement for Feisal's approval. France would recognize Syrian independence. In return, France would supply all the advisers, the new state would be a federation of local autonomies, and Feisal would acknowledge France's contribution to Syrian history, such as the 1860 landing of French troops at Beirut which saved the Christians.[25] Feisal, following Lawrence's recommendations, rejected the proposed accord. On April 19 Feisal demanded complete independence for Syria "without conditions or reservations." French participation would be limited to supplying technical specialists.[26] Realizing that France would never accept these terms, Feisal informed Clemenceau the next day that he was returning to Syria. He facetiously thanked Clemenceau for having been the first to support the sending of an inquiry commission to the Middle East.[27] Lawrence and Feisal were obviously betting that the results of the forthcoming Inquiry Commission and continued British assistance would keep France out of Syria.

The failure of the discussions surprised France. Pichon had become convinced that Feisal had initiated the discussions because of British pressure. The French minister of foreign affairs believed that Lloyd George was finally going to honor his December, 1918, pledge to Clemenceau and thereby allow France a free hand in Syria. It was thought that Great Britain sought an immediate understanding between Feisal and France in order to prevent the forthcoming and potentially dangerous trip of the Inquiry Commission to Mesopotamia. Pichon thought that as a first step France would assume payment of all subsidies to Feisal and French troops would replace Allenby's forces in Syria. Feisal's intransigence, however, made it apparent to Pichon that Lloyd George was still reneging on his December promise to Clemenceau.[28]

England, in all probability, had attempted to play the "honest broker" between France and Feisal.[29] Feisal may have considered proposals put forth by Alfred Milner as the basis of his recent negotiations with France. Lord Milner, British colonial secretary, had suggested to Lloyd George in early March a basis for a possible understanding between France and Feisal. The basic premises of Milner's plan were that it was useless "trying to diddle the French out of Syria" and that France could not "get hold" of Syria if Feisal continued his opposition. A compromise was needed. Milner proposed that France should give up all attempts of "bossing Feisal in the sense of full administrative control such as they exercise in Tunis and Morocco." Feisal, in return, would accept the French mandate for Syria. However, it would be "the mildest form of mandate." It should resemble

something like what was contemplated in the Sykes-Picot agreement for the "A" and "B" areas, namely, "priority of right of enterprise of local loans" for the mandatory power, and the appointment only of such functionaries as Feisal may ask for. These functionaries would probably be confined to Public Works and Finance. What this means is that the material development of the country would be undertaken by the French. The railways, ports and other public works would be run by them, while the administration otherwise would be substantially native.

Milner doubted that France would accept anything less than the "virtual ownership of Syria." However, "if the pill were sweetened," France might accept his proposals. Specifically, Milner recommended that France be given total control of Lebanon and the port of Alexandretta.[30] Milner's basic pessimism about his proposals was well founded. The recent discussions between Feisal and France revealed that possession of Lebanon and Alexandretta would not satisfy France's colonial desires. Only Syria could do that.

The collapse of the recent discussions raised an important question. Where would France go from here? Robert de Caix argued that the "keys" to Syria had to be wrested from England.[31] It would be useless to continue further negotiations with Feisal. De Caix maintained that, if an agreement were reached with Feisal, it could not last. French policy in Syria was based on encouraging the particularistic elements within the confines of a federation. The recent discussions with Feisal had demonstrated unequivocally that he was an ambitious nationalist intent on driving France out of Syria and Lebanon, while creating a large unitary state. France had never before encountered a colonial leader of this type. Indeed, France would not find in Feisal "the stuff of a Bey of Tunisia."[32]

Nevertheless, Pichon instructed Picot, French high

---

[24] Kaddour Ben Chabrit, aide to De Caix, "Note de Kaddour Ben Chabrit," Apr. 14, 1919, ibid., vol. 12, fol. 22.

[25] The proposed agreement is entitled "Declaration," Apr. 17, 1919, AAE, série: Levant, Arabie-Hedjaz, vol. 4, fols. 36–37. For Clemenceau's covering letter, see Clemenceau to Feisal, Apr. 17, 1919, ibid., fol. 85.

[26] Feisal to Clemenceau, Apr. 19, 1919, AAE, série: Levant S-L-C, vol. 12, fols. 133–134.

[27] Feisal to Clemenceau, Apr. 20, 1919, AAE, série: Levant, Arabie-Hedjaz, vol. 4, fol. 104.

[28] Pichon to P. Cambon, May 4, 1919, AMG, 5N 76, dossier: Asie Mineure, Turquie.

[29] Poincaré to Pichon, Mar. 30, 1919, in: Raymond Poincaré, Au service de la France: neuf années de souvenirs (11 v., Paris, 1926–1974) 11: p. 296.

[30] Milner to Lloyd George, Mar. 8, 1919, quoted in Lloyd George, 1939: 2: pp. 679–680.

[31] De Caix to Clemenceau, Apr. 22, 1919, AAE, série: Levant, Arabie-Hedjaz, vol. 4, fols. 117–118.

[32] "Rapport de R. de Caix à Pichon," Apr. 22, 1919, AAE, série: Levant S-L-C, vol. 12, fols. 121–130.

commissioner to Lebanon, to continue negotiating with Feisal. The basis of the French position, however, remained unchanged and uncompromising: French military occupation of Syria and effective control of the state.[33] Clearly the Quai d'Orsay did not appreciate the extent and scope of Moslem fears concerning the possible implementation of a French mandate. In Damascus an ever-increasing number of political clubs, feeding on xenophobia, pan-Islamic, and pan-Arab nationalism, denounced French intentions to obtain the Syrian mandate.[34] And in Lebanon, French administrative methods were alienating the Moslems. A French official recorded that "the cause of the reservation with which the Moslem element regards us lies in the apprehension it feels from the possible application in Syria of our North African administrative methods." More specifically:

All the important posts [in Lebanon] such as governors of the big cities and the districts, as well as the heads of the main administrative services, are in fact now occupied by our [French] officers and the country finds itself submitted to a government of direct administration similar to that of our [French] military territories in Algeria, without even having the satisfaction of native representation. . . .

Paris was warned that the perpetuation of this condition, in an age of increased nationalism and Wilsonian idealism could only result in "danger for the French cause in the Levant."[35]

Feisal's counterproposals were also unrealistic. He did not want to reach an agreement. Although demonstrating "outward friendship to France, [Feisal] is as bitterly opposed to them as ever and he insists that if they remain in Syria or get any sort of mandate he will fight them to the last."[36] He was supremely confident that the forthcoming Inquiry Commission and continued British assistance could keep France out of Syria. Thus, he told Picot in two late May meetings in Damascus that before he would consent to a French mandate, French troops must abandon Lebanon and that Syrians, not France, must rule Syria. Feisal also demanded that Lebanon as well as Mosul and Palestine be included in a "Greater Syria."[37] These demands were farfetched because France had already agreed that England should control postwar Palestine and Mosul. Furthermore, Picot understood, if Feisal did not, that France would have great difficulty in persuading Lebanon to join Feisal's "Greater Syria." During the late spring of 1919 the Lebanese Maronites, led by the patriarch, actively protested against any kind of political union with Syria. The Catholics, rejecting membership in the French-sponsored Syrian federation, demanded that France protect a "Greater Lebanon."[38] A besieged Picot beseeched the Maronites to stop the public demonstrations. The demonstrations threatened to undermine French policy. If France were to recognize an independent "Greater Lebanon," the Moslems would rebel and all chance of a rapprochement with Feisal would have been destroyed. Picot did not believe that his pleas for moderation would be followed because "in a region where private interests prevail over general interests, it is to be feared that I would have trouble making the voice of reason heard."[39] The unsympathetic General Gilbert Clayton, director of British Military Intelligence in Cairo, correctly observed that "it is not easy to appreciate the lines which the policy of French officials in this area is now following in this complicated situation. They are faced with the difficulty of having to conciliate Emir Feisal and the Arabs at Damascus without alienating the traditional support of the Maronite Christians, the majority of whom are members of the party which desires an independent Lebanon."[40]

All the frustrations arising from France's failure to resolve the Syrian problem burst forth in late May when Clemenceau, Lloyd George, and Woodrow Wilson once again met in Paris. When Lloyd George suggested that France receive a provisional mandate over Syria pending the report of the Inquiry Commission, Clemenceau accused the prime minister of duplicity. To have accepted Lloyd George's offer would have meant that France would never control Syria. Instead, Clemenceau announced that France would not cooperate with the Inquiry Commission until French troops were permitted to occupy Syria. Clemenceau pointed out that contrary to his December 2, 1918, understanding with Lloyd George, France had not yet received Syria. France nevertheless had sanctioned British control of Mosul and Palestine. The French premier also denounced the frequent British attempts to expand the northern Palestinian border deep into Syria; the British sought an enlarged Palestine in order to control and protect

---

[33] Memo by Jean Goût, "Occupation de la Syrie-Cilicie," May 19, 1919, AAE, série: Papiers d'agent: André Tardieu, carton 53, dossier: Syrie.

[34] See Picot to Pichon, Mar. 1, 4, 20, 1920, AMG, 6N 193; Colonel Edouard Cousse, French military attaché in Damascus, to Picot, Feb. 21, Mar. 17, 19, 30, 1919, AAE, série: Levant, Arabie-Hedjaz, vol. 4, fols. 59-61, 63-64, 68-70, 72-74.

[35] Charles Feer, Picot's assistant in Beirut, to Pichon, Apr. 18, 1919, AMG, 6N 193, dossier: 1919; Gontaut-Biron, 1922: p. 274.

[36] Allenby to General Henry Wilson, chief of the Imperial General Staff, May 14, 1919, F.O. 371/4180, 2117/74825.

[37] Picot to Pichon, May 22, 1919, AMG, 6N 80, dossier: Syrie-Hedjaz; Picot to Pichon, May 29, 1919, AMG, 6N 193, dossier: 1919.

[38] "Greater Lebanon" would have included the eastern region of Bekaa.

[39] Picot to Pichon, May 15, 1919, AMG, 6N 193, dossier: 1919. See also Picot to Pichon, June 28, 1919, ibid.

[40] Clayton to Curzon, June 23, 1919, F.O. 371/4181, 2117/98129.

the major railway routes from the Mediterranean to Mesopotamia. If France were ever to gain control of Syria, Clemenceau wanted something more than a strip of land stretching from Damascus to Aleppo.

To all this criticism Lloyd George responded as he did in March: when France agreed to the Sykes-Picot agreement, it had agreed to the establishment of an independent Syria. The Sykes-Picot agreement, according to the British interpretation, meant that France "possesses no right east of Lebanon; it cannot put its flag there and it cannot send one single soldier there." Clemenceau ended the discussion by warning Lloyd George:

> The primary purpose that we have the duty of preserving is that of the common interest of the Entente. What I shall tell you frankly is that I shall not continue in any way whatsoever to enter into a partnership with you in this part of the world if our mutual agreements are not upheld. ... It is up to Great Britain to decide what she will do. As for me, I no longer have anything to say.[41]

The wartime alliance was coming apart at the seams and, as a result, France's position in the Middle East never appeared less secure. France could not accept Lloyd George's interpretation of the Sykes-Picot agreement. To do so would have been tantamount to formal recognition that France had emerged from the war prepared to play a subordinate role to Great Britain. Clemenceau agreed with André Tardieu's bitter observation that "too many Englishmen have failed to recognize that France, bleeding and plundered, is entitled to something better than daily advice to renounce her rights."[42] If the alliance were to survive, England would have to make the necessary concessions.

4. APPARENT SUCCESS

France's moderate and conservative political parties overwhelmingly supported Pichon's Middle Eastern policies. As the Paris peace conference convened in January, 1919, the *Correspondance d'Orient* presented the core of France's Middle Eastern policy: "It is simply a question of stating that the moral and material interests of France in Syria are greater than those of the other European powers, that this domination must be maintained, and that no other nation should be allowed to oppose it."[1] That included the Hejaz and the Sherifians. The prestigious and usually temperate *Le Temps* denounced the Sherifians' attempt to rule Syria: "The policy of the Hejaz ... seems like a vast undertaking at annexation, like the substitution of Bedouin imperialism for Turkish imperialism. The doctrine of Arab unity is serving the ambitions of a little clique of Arab or European conquistadors. ..."[2] The Arab, "whatever the level of his development may be, is obviously not able to perform the most elementary duty of self-rule: the maintenance of domestic order." Thus, the responsibility of the peace conference was clear: "Premature independence should not be given these underdeveloped people. ... They should be prepared for independence through gradual political education, which would vary according to the character of each Protector Power."[3] The ultra-Catholic *La Croix* urged England to support France's plans for Syria: "We have too much confidence in the honesty of our Allies to believe that they will give themselves up to the dream of Anglo-Bedouin imperialism and believe that they will recognize France's authority in ... Syria. ..."[4]

French criticism of England became more harsh and shrill by mid-1919 when it became apparent that England was blocking French aspirations in Syria. *L'Asie française* bitterly condemned Great Britain for having created, "through the systematic development of a virulent nationalism, an environment in Syria which makes the assignment of the Syrian mandate to France difficult and even impossible." England, an "insatiable imperialist," was playing a dangerous game in fostering Syrian nationalism. Arab nationalism could not only be used against the French in Syria, but also against the British in Mesopotamia and Egypt.[5]

If these midyear press attacks reflected the sentiments of an important segment of the Quai d'Orsay and the French Cabinet,[6] Georges Leygues, minister of the navy, did not believe that the press campaign was adequate. He argued that, if England and the Sherifians succeeded in keeping France out of the Middle East, France's strategic position in the Medi-

---

[41] "Conversation entre M. le Président Wilson, M. Lloyd George et M. Clemenceau," May 21, 22, 1919, AAE, série: Levant S-L-C, vol. 13, fols. 51–70. See also "Notes of a Meeting Held May 22, 1919, at 11 A.M.," USFR 5: pp. 807–811; Paul Mantoux, *Les Délibérations du conseil des quatre: 24 mars–28 juin 1919* (2 v., Paris, 1955) 2: pp. 159–164.

[42] André Tardieu, *The Truth about the Treaty* (Indianapolis, 1921), p. 447. Clemenceau wrote the introduction to Tardieu's book. Tardieu served in the French delegation at the peace conference.

[1] *Correspondance d'Orient*, no. 205 (Jan. 15, 1919): p. 23. See also *L'Action française*, Jan. 6, 1919. For a summary of early 1919 French press reaction to the Syrian question, see Pierre Miquel, *La Paix de Versailles et l'opinion publique française* (Paris, 1972), pp. 497–501.

[2] *Le Temps*, Feb. 11, 1919. See also *Correspondance d'Orient*, no. 208 (Feb. 28, 1919): pp. 146–153.

[3] *Le Temps*, May 4, 1919. See also *ibid.*, Mar. 25, 1919.

[4] *La Croix*, Feb. 25, 1919. See also *Le Temps*, Feb. 26, 1919; *L'Asie française*, no. 174 (Oct., 1918–Jan., 1919).

[5] *L'Asie française*, no. 175 (Feb.–July, 1919): pp. 170, 173. See also *Correspondance d'Orient*, no. 215 (June 15, 1919): pp. 481–488; articles by Jacques Bainville, *L'Action française*, Aug. 3, Sept. 5, 1919; *Le Temps*, Aug. 23, Sept. 8, 1919.

[6] Pichon to Balfour, July 28, 1919, attached to letter Balfour to Curzon, July 28, 1919, BD, 1st series, vol. 4, no. 230, pp. 321–322.

terranean would be irreparably damaged. Furthermore, if denied a power base in the Middle East, France would have no easy access to her Pacific colonies. France, Leygues strongly recommended, "must clearly affirm her rights, not through words, to which no one pays heed, but through action."[7]

Veteran French diplomats, on the other hand, were shocked by the outburst against England. Camille Barrère, French ambassador to Italy, warned Pichon that "the alliance with England must be the cornerstone of our policy on the condition of reciprocity. And I know full well how much our strength and our security depend upon this entente."[8] And Joseph de Fleuriau in London observed that

the entente cordiale . . . will not survive if Syria takes over in today's public opinion the place formerly occupied by Egypt. That is all the more serious because there are many English who want a rapprochement with Germany and the number of those who will confess their pro-German feelings will quickly grow after the final peace settlement.[9]

Clemenceau felt uncomfortable with the public outburst against France's closest ally. Yet, France's position in the Middle East had been sabotaged by Great Britain. He told Lloyd George's aide in early September that

France . . . had always played a great part there [Middle East], and from the economic point of view a settlement which would give France economic opportunities was essential, especially in view of their present financial condition. . . . French public opinion expected a settlement which was consonant with France's position. . . . If unity [between France and Great Britain] were to be maintained, it was necessary to clear up all these outstanding questions, and in order to do this England must help France to a just settlement in accordance with her historical rights and her economic and political necessities in the Middle East.[10]

The British were also concerned by the deteriorating situation. When the English government asked Pichon to put "the soft pedal down upon this loud anti-British campaign," the French foreign minister, reflecting Clemenceau's sentiments, emphasized that he "saw no means of succeeding in so doing unless he were helped by us [England]; both sides must do something and not only the French government."[11] Lord Balfour was sympathetic to the French plea. However, in early August, when he once again reviewed Britain's wartime understandings with the Arabs and the French, he concluded that "France, England, and America have got themselves into a position over the Syrian problem so inextricably confused that no really neat and satisfactory issue is now possible for any of them."[12] The heart of the problem was the difficulty in reconciling Britain's "quasi-territorial ambitions" with French "ambitions." "Neither of us," observed Balfour, "wants much less than supreme economic and political control, to be exercised no doubt in friendly and unostentatious co-operation with the Arabs—but nevertheless, in the last resort, to be exercised."[13]

Lord Grey, British foreign minister at the time the Sykes-Picot agreement had been arranged, strongly told Balfour that there was a solution to the French-British impasse. Grey claimed that McMahon's pledges to Hussein and the Sykes-Picot agreement were not incompatible. Britain had promised Hussein an independent Arabia whereas the Sykes-Picot agreement had reserved Syria for France. He told Balfour that "it was perfectly open to us, without any engagement to the King of Hedjaz, to come out of Syria after the Armistice was signed and let the French take our place."[14]

Lloyd George, however, continued to believe that the Sykes-Picot agreement had created an independent Syria. Furthermore, he wanted to honor what he considered to be British wartime obligations to the Arabs.[15] At the same time, the British prime minister was seeking a method to appease France. He believed that he had found a formula for his quandry. On September 13 Lloyd George informed Clemenceau that British troops would soon evacuate Syria, Lebanon, and Cilicia. The British garrisons in Syria, that is, east of the Sykes-Picot line, would be given to Feisal while the garrisons west of the line—Lebanon—were to be given to France.[16] Lloyd George had met one of Clemenceau's frequent requests: British troops were to be removed from Syria.

---

[7] Leygues to Pichon, Aug. 16, 1919, Archives Marine, Ea 201, dossier: Mai à août, 1919.

[8] Barrère to Pichon, Aug. 28, 1919, AAE, série: Levant S-L-C, vol. 17, fol. 59.

[9] Fleuriau, French chargé d'affaires, to Pichon, Aug. 19, 1919, *ibid.*, vol. 16, fol. 191.

[10] Philip Kerr to Lloyd George, Sept. 12, 1919, Lloyd George Papers, F/51/1/40. Kerr was Lloyd George's private secretary.

[11] George Grahame, British chargé d'affaires in Paris, to Curzon, acting secretary of state for foreign affairs, Aug. 12, 1919, F.O. 371/4182, 2117/116079. See also Grahame to Curzon, July 27, 1919, BD, 1st series, vol. 4, no. 229, p. 321.

[12] Memo by Balfour, Aug. 11, 1919, BD, 1st series, vol. 4, no. 242, p. 342. See also Balfour memorandum for Lloyd George, June 26, 1919, included in Balfour to Curzon, July 2, 1919, *ibid.*, no. 211, p. 301.

[13] Memo by Balfour, "Some Difficulties to be Borne in Mind in any Syrian Negotiations," Sept. 9, 1919, *ibid.*, no. 265, pp. 373–374.

[14] Memo enclosed in Grey to Balfour, Sept. 9, 1919, Lloyd George Papers, F/12/1/43.

[15] Meeting between Lloyd George and Feisal, Sept. 19, 1919, F.O. 371/4237, 131418/132929.

[16] Lloyd George, "Aide Mémoire," Sept. 13, 1919, AAE, série: Levant S-L-C, vol. 17, fols. 218–219. The removal of British troops from Syria was also connected to the accelerated demobilization of Britain's armed forces. All available troops were needed to keep the postwar peace within the British empire: Mesopotamia, Egypt, India, and Ireland (Nevakivi, 1969: p. 185).

How would France respond to this latest British initiative? To have accepted England's September 13 proposal would have meant that, although France would have had the Syrian mandate, Feisal would have been in control of Syria. The other possibilities for France were almost as bleak. Paris could have accepted Feisal's terms for a Franco-Syrian agreement. France would be a powerless mandatory for Syria, Lebanon, and Palestine. This would have brought France into conflict with the Lebanese Christians, Zionists, and the British. A third possibility would have been to create an Arab confederation comprised of Syria, Lebanon, Palestine, and Mesopotamia. England and France would have held a joint mandate over this confederation. The British partnership in this scheme, it was argued, would encourage Feisal to accept more readily the French presence. The major drawback to this plan, however, was the fear that England and France would be involved in frequent and interminable squabbles over the Arab question. A last possibility would have been for Clemenceau to have insisted, as he had done in the past, that France would adhere only to the Sykes-Picot agreement. As previously interpreted by Clemenceau, this meant total French control of Syria. Such a policy entailed certain risks. If French troops moved into Syria, Feisal might have resisted. A war against Feisal, no matter how short, would have alienated England and might have sparked an Arab rebellion in France's North African colonies.[17]

Clemenceau once again insisted on the sanctity of the Sykes-Picot agreement. On October 9 he reminded Lloyd George that England occupied Mesopotamia. Therefore, France should be able to occupy Syria. As a mandatory, how could France guarantee order in Syria if denied access to that country?[18] A week later Lloyd George responded sympathetically. The prime minister explained that Feisal would be going to Paris in order to "come to terms with the French government direct." Feisal, without British troops serving as a buffer between himself and France, would be more receptive to an agreement with France. However, Lloyd George warned that Feisal would not be a sacrificial lamb. The British prime minister cautioned Clemenceau that Feisal should be treated "with the courtesy and consideration which one of the Allies deserves." Lloyd George emphasized that

his Majesty's Government cannot conceal the anxiety they have felt at the apparent determination of the French press to deal with the Emir Feisal and the Arab problem with a high hand. If this were indeed the policy of the French Government, the British Government are afraid that it would inevitably lead to serious and long-continued disturbances throughout the Arab territories which might easily spread to the whole Mohammedan world. The Emir Feisal is now anxious to cooperate with the Allies. They earnestly hope that during the course of the negotiations in Paris nothing will occur to drive the Emir Feisal into hostility or induce him to enter into relations with those hostile elements which exist in the Middle East, and are the enemies alike of France and Britain.[19]

Clemenceau was now convinced that Lloyd George had made the necessary concessions. He told the British prime minister in early November that

you gave us the proof of your intentions when . . . you took responsibility for the relief of the British troops by French troops, and that you advised him [Feisal] to come here to reach an understanding with the French Government.
If this procedure had been followed at once at the beginning, that is to say, at the time of the occupation of Damascus a year ago, the recent misunderstandings would without doubt have been avoided. I am pleased to think that henceforth there is no chance of their recurring between us. . . .[20]

Clemenceau, supported by Philippe Berthelot and Jean Goût at the Quai d'Orsay, now began to weave a new Syrian policy, one which would attempt to satisfy the French colonialists, protect French imperial interests, and, at the same time, gain the support of Feisal and Great Britain.

In October, Clemenceau had appointed General Henri Gouraud high commissioner to Syria and Lebanon. Gouraud was a conservative Catholic who had been a wartime hero and had prewar experience as a colonial administrator in Morocco and Mauritania. His appointment had been interpreted to mean that France was going to impose her will upon Feisal. In reality, however, Gouraud had been appointed to appease the French Right, not to prepare Feisal's removal.

Almost immediately Clemenceau and Gouraud clashed. Lloyd George's September 13 note had promised that France could replace British troops west of the Sykes-Picot line. This included the Bekaa region in eastern Lebanon. However, Clemenceau in November decided that, at least temporarily, French troops would not occupy the Bekaa. In return, he expected the Sherifian troops to evacuate the area. Gouraud immediately criticized Clemenceau's decision. The general argued that Clemenceau's gesture would be interpreted by the Arabs as a sign of French weakness, thereby encouraging

---

[17] All of these possibilities are discussed in Marie-Xavier Laforcade, Picot's assistant in Lebanon, to Pichon, Sept. 14, 1919, AAE, série: Levant, 1918–1929, Palestine, vol. 2, fols. 93–95.

[18] Clemenceau to Curzon, Oct. 9, 1919, BD, 1st series, vol. 4, no. 314, p. 453.

[19] Lloyd George to Clemenceau, Oct. 18, 1919, *ibid.*, no. 334, pp. 486–487.

[20] Clemenceau to Lloyd George, Nov. 9, 1919, *ibid.*, no. 357, pp. 520–521.

Feisal to resist more energetically French diplomatic advances.[21]

The willingness to forego the immediate occupation of Bekaa, Clemenceau retorted, was "striking proof of the loyalty of our intentions toward the Arabs and of the moderation of our policy. . . . Far from hurting us, these steps assure the success of our Syrian action and that [has been accomplished] without violence, which could have had repercussions both within our country and abroad."[22] Clemenceau was satisfied that England's decision of September 13 to evacuate Syria had restored French prestige in the Middle East. Now Clemenceau wanted the friendship and cooperation of Feisal and Great Britain:

> Once there is an agreement with Feisal, it will evidently be in our interest to build up his importance and put our trust in him: the English have had Feisal accepted by the conference as the qualified representative of the Arabs and have urged us to get along with him. We could have either gotten rid of him or played a role in accord with him: this latter solution protected us from any disagreements with our Allies; that is the one I chose.[23]

Only a few months earlier, in June, 1919, Feisal had told the Inquiry Commission that he favored an American or British mandate for Syria. He had totally rejected the possibility of a French mandate.[24] Placed in a more vulnerable position by Lloyd George's September decision to remove British troops from Syria, Feisal went to Paris in October in an attempt to reach an understanding with Clemenceau. The ensuing discussions centered on France's role as the mandatory power. The basic question focused on the question of sovereignty. Was power to lie with the French or the Syrians? In her initial proposal of December 6 France offered Feisal nothing less than total French control of Syria. Although France promised to recognize "the right of the Syrian people to self-government as an independent nation," France intended to control completely the country's foreign affairs, its judiciary, economic, and political life. Not surprisingly, Feisal rejected this program.[25]

On December 16 Jean Goût, chief of the Asian Department at the Quai d'Orsay, offered a new proposal to Feisal, one with major concessions. France, which was to have a monopoly on Syria's large-scale loans and economic undertakings, would supply the military and civil administrators. However, these technicians would be responsible to the Syrian government. France agreed to permit Syria to have a parliament. The Syrian parliament would have sole power to make the laws, determine the taxes, and "exercise all the rights enjoyed by the parliament of the civilized nations." The Arabic language, not Turkish or French, would be the official language of the country. Finally, France was prepared to recognize Feisal as chief of a united Syria. Feisal, in return, would agree that Syria be a French mandate.[26]

Feisal and France reached a tentative agreement on January 6, 1920. The January 6 agreement contained most of the basic clauses of the December 16 proposal. However, the January 6 agreement clarified and elaborated certain aspects of the December 16 program: "The investiture [of French advisers] and their powers of authority will be determined by common consent of the two governments in an agreement specifying the duration and obligations of their mission." In addition, the January 6 agreement, which was provisional until Feisal could gain popular support for the French mandate, stipulated that an independent Lebanon would be under a French mandate. France would set Syria's foreign policy and sponsor Syria's entrance into the League of Nations. French troops would be stationed in Cilicia and could be deployed in the interior of Syria only with the consent of the Syrian government.[27]

The January 6 agreement, which Feisal termed "a small trusteeship of France,"[28] was accepted by Feisal because the integrity of Syria had been preserved, French troops would not be in Syria or in Lebanon, and Syrians would have some control over much of the country's political, legal, and administrative apparatus. Clemenceau had granted these concessions because he could not afford to alienate Great Britain, whose friendship was essential for France's security. British aid and cooperation would also be needed in the postwar reconstruction of Europe. Secondly, Clemenceau saw no need to provoke a rebellion in Syria, thereby forcing a war-weary France to pour large amounts of men and money into the Mid-

---

[21] Gouraud to Pichon, Nov. 29, 1919, AMG, 6N 193, dossier: Télégrammes du général Gouraud.

[22] Clemenceau to Gouraud, Nov. 30, 1919, AMG, 6N 291, dossier: Divers, Levant 1919–1921.

[23] Clemenceau to Gouraud, Dec. 9, 1919, AAE, série: Levant, 1918–1929, Arabie, vol. 7, fol. 254.

[24] The Inquiry Commission, known as the King-Crane Commission, went to Syria in the summer of 1919. It never went to Mesopotamia. It reported that the Christians wanted a French mandate. The Moslems, however, wanted independence. If this were not granted the Moslems would accept the United States or Great Britain as the mandatory power. The report was never considered by the peace conference, and the text was not made public until 1922.

[25] "Projet d'accord franco-arabe," Dec. 6, 1919, AAE, série: Levant S-L-C, vol. 20, fol. 249.

[26] Jean Goût's draft submitted to Feisal, Dec. 16, 1919, ibid., fols. 247–248.

[27] "L'Accord provisoire du 6 janvier 1920," AAE, série: Levant 1918–1929, Arabie, vol. 8, fols. 83–86. For the text, see Appendix 2.

[28] Gouraud to Millerand, Jan. 25, 1920, AAE, série: Levant S-L-C, vol. 22, fol. 3.

dle East.[29] The January 6 accord recognized in limited degree the Wilsonian ideals of self-determination, protected France's prestige and economic interests, satisfied the Catholics in Lebanon and France, and did not threaten British imperial interests. The agreement was based on common interest, moderation, and moral purpose.

Instant dangers to the mutually beneficial French-Feisal agreement abounded everywhere. The nationalists in Damascus were gaining ground. Gouraud reported that the Arab nationalists "see no reason to be submitted to Feisal now that he accepts the collaboration with France which he had for so long vehemently repudiated. Some extremists repudiate Feisal as a traitor and the others find him incapable of forming a policy of rapprochement with France."[30] Gouraud strongly recommended that Feisal remain in Paris because "whatever his talents and his sincerity may be, it is to be feared that if he disembarks before the state of things is restored, he will be fatally caught up by the [Nationalist] movement of which he would become the head which it still lacks."[31]

Philippe Berthelot, chief of the Political Division at the Quai d'Orsay, disagreed. He believed that Feisal was strong enough to control the nationalists:

> The return [to Syria] of Emir Feisal, who is in agreement with us on the essential points, is going to help in the repression of that banditry born from the war and favored by some hot-head politicians and is going to demonstrate the falseness of the accusations levelled against our policy of association with the natives and of respect for their liberties.[32]

Clemenceau concurred that Feisal's immediate return to Damascus "to act in collaboration with [France] is indispensable; if not, incidents are going to increase without us being able to find in Damascus even a really responsible authority, sincerely desirous of collaboration and capable of being obeyed."[33] Now that France had made major concessions, Clemenceau expected from Feisal "corresponding loyalty on his part, and that the absolute respect of his authority by his followers must satisfy me." If these two conditions were not met, the French government "would impose order and respect of its rights through force...."[34]

Feisal, upon whom Clemenceau was basing his policy, was not altogether confident that the January 6 understanding could be the basis of a permanent agreement between France and Syria. The news that Syrian nationalists were attacking French troops left him shaken and "apprehensive about the future." Feisal also feared General Gouraud because the general's "attitude ... is the opposite of the policy of assistance and support that Syria expects from France." Feisal believed that "many of the officers in Gouraud's entourage have no other goal than the conquest of the country.... [They] expect that local military disturbances or incidents will give them an excuse to occupy Damascus."[35]

Feisal's apprehension was well founded. De Caix, recently appointed to Gouraud's staff as a civilian adviser, believed that the January 6 accord was a disaster for France. De Caix claimed that the January accord had given too much power to the Syrian parliament. Feisal and Arab nationalism had been strengthened. Syrian nationalism could be broken only if Syria were divided into cantons; Nossayris, Metawlis, Druzes, Shiites, Sunnis, Christians, and Jews should live in separate political and administrative districts. De Caix was also concerned that, if particularism did not prevent the creation of a unitary Syrian state, a nationalist leader such as Feisal could serve as a rallying point against France's position in Moslem North Africa. De Caix solemnly warned the Quai d'Orsay: "It is ... through an African perspective that we should consider our Eastern policy."[36] De Caix further cautioned that, if the January 6 accord were fulfilled, France would soon be eased out of Syria. If such were to happen, not only would "another [foreign] power assume our place [in Syria]," but world opinion would consider France a "finished people," destroyed financially, militarily, and psychologically by the Great War.[37]

Similar sentiments were shared by a segment of the Quai d'Orsay. The January 6 accord was considered defective for several reasons. The French advisers would, in reality, have little power. Secondly, France had agreed to sponser Syria's entry into the League of Nations; yet, the Syrian representative to the League would inevitably use the international forum to criticize France. Lastly, French, not Arabic, should be the language of Syria. How else could France preserve her cultural domination?[38]

But perhaps the biggest threat to the fulfillment

---

[29] Lord Derby to Curzon, Dec. 2, 1919, Lloyd George Papers, F/12/2/8.

[30] Gouraud to Pichon, Dec. 29, 1919, AMG, 6N 193, dossier: Télégrammes du général Gouraud.

[31] Gouraud to Pichon, Dec. 17, 1919, *ibid.*

[32] Berthelot to Jusserand, Jan. 17, 1920, AAE, série: Levant S-L-C, vol. 21, fol. 239.

[33] Clemenceau to Gouraud, Jan. 8, 1920, *ibid.*, fols. 103–104.

[34] Clemenceau to Gouraud, Jan. 7, 1920, AMG, 6N 194.

[35] Memo by Khaddour Ben Ghabut, "Conversation avec l'Emir Feysal," Jan. 9, 1920, AAE série: Levant S-L-C, vol. 20, fols. 141–142.

[36] Twenty-eight page memo by Robert de Caix, "Note sur la politique de l'accord avec Feysal," Jan. 26, 1920, *ibid.*, vol. 22, fol. 71; see also fols. 50–77.

[37] Memo by De Caix, "Esquisse de l'organisation de la Syrie sous le mandat français," July 17, 1920, *ibid.*, vol. 31, fol. 28.

[38] Quai d'Orsay memo, "Note sur l'accord provisoire avec l'Emir Feysal," Jan. 30, 1920, *ibid.*, vol. 22, fols. 136–147.

of the January 6 accord was Clemenceau's sudden resignation two weeks later. "Had M. Clemenceau remained in office another twelve months," Lloyd George soberly recalled two decades later, "I am convinced all would have gone well."[39] Part of the reason for Clemenceau's resignation can be attributed to the French national elections of November, 1919. The newly elected Chamber of Deputies was more intensely Catholic, nationalistic, and imperialistic than the preceding one had been. The French elections, as those in Great Britain and the United States, constituted a repudiation of Wilsonian principles. Clemenceau's successor as premier, Alexandre Millerand, would reflect the prevailing postwar mood. Consequently, there would be little sympathy for the aspirations of the colonial Moslem population.

5. ROAD TO DAMASCUS

When Alexandre Millerand became French premier and foreign minister in January, 1920, he unenthusiastically accepted Clemenceau's January 6 provisional accord with Feisal. This agreement stipulated that France would receive the mandate for Syria and Lebanon. France would supply the technical advisers to Syria as well as control her foreign and financial policies. In return, France recognized a unitary Syrian state and, in restricted fashion, the right of self-determination for the Syrian people. Millerand believed that France had made the major concessions; therefore, he was impatient that Feisal fulfill his part of the bargain: to persuade the Syrians to accept the French mandate, to restore order, and to force the Syrians to cease guerilla warfare against French troops. Millerand informed General Gouraud in early February that the January 6 accord required of Feisal

proof that he is capable of being obeyed by the Arabs on all occasions . . . so that our agreements are respected to the mutual benefit of all parties concerned. . . . He has to offer more complete proof of his ability to impose his authority; if this were not forthcoming, we ourselves would be authorized to take any measures necessary for the maintenance of order, the defense of the people, and the safety of our troops. . . . Regarding the Sherifians, you certainly possess the means of imposing respect for our rights.[1]

Gouraud responded gloomily that Feisal was being buffeted by nationalists who sought total Syrian independence: "Though Feisal is sincere, he is now absolutely incapable of being in control of the situation. Thus the agreements that he made with us in Paris obviously lose much of [their] importance. . . ."[2]

Reacting to this intense pressure from the Syrian nationalists, Feisal on February 21, 1920, asked Millerand to change or clarify certain aspects of the January 6 agreement. Specifically, Feisal wanted France to state categorically that the proposed French advisers would only advise and not implement policy, that the future Lebanon state would not include the Bekaa region, and that Syria would have some control over its foreign policy. Equally disturbing to Paris was Feisal's declaration that he would refuse to discuss a Middle East settlement unless France and Great Britain promised complete independence to the Arabs in Syria, Palestine, and Mesopotamia.[3]

Millerand refused Feisal's requests. France could not "agree, under [the threat of] extremists, to additional concessions to Feisal, to whom we have stated that the fulfillment and continuation of our provisional agreement were dependent upon his loyal willingness . . . to carry out his part of the agreement." By late February, at a time when Feisal sought further concessions, Millerand's position was hardening. The French premier believed that the January 6 accord needed to be revised. But the revisions were not the same as those sought by Feisal. Millerand believed that a final solution to the Syrian question should give France "greater and more flexible rights and means than the French plan [January 6 accord] made with Feisal."[4] The kind of extended prerogatives that Millerand had in mind were to be achieved by reintroducing the notion of "autonomies." Whereas the Feisal-Clemenceau accord of January 6 had recognized a unitary Syrian state, Millerand in early March advocated that Syria be split into several groups; the divisions would follow traditional ethnic and confessional lines.[5]

Ever since his return to Syria in January, 1920, Feisal had been vascillating between the necessity to seek an agreement with France and the demand of the Syrian nationalists to proclaim complete independence from France. By early March, Feisal's options had been greatly narrowed: to support the French mandate and sanction the use of French troops to crush the nationalists; to abandon his role as leader of the Syrians; or to join the nationalists against France. He selected the last course. On March 7 and 8 the Syrian General Congress, claiming to represent the Syrians and Lebanese, met in Damascus and proclaimed complete independence for Syria, including Palestine. Feisal was proclaimed king of

---

[39] Lloyd George, 2 (1939): p. 711.
[1] Millerand to Gouraud, Feb. 10, 1920, AAE, série: Levant S-L-C, vol. 23, fol. 58. See also Millerand to Gouraud, AAE, série: Levant, Arabie, vol. 9, fol. 12.
[2] Gouraud to Millerand, Feb. 18, 1920, AAE, série: Levant S-L-C, vol. 23, fol. 187.
[3] Gouraud to Millerand, Feb. 21, 1920, ibid., vol. 24, fols. 3–4.
[4] Millerand to Gouraud, Feb. 25, 1920, ibid., fol. 55.
[5] Millerand to Gouraud, Mar. 7, 1920, ibid., fol. 197.

Syria, Lebanon, and Palestine. Feisal's brother, Abdullah, was proclaimed king of an independent Iraq.[6]

France and Great Britain had been presented with a *fait accompli*. One other thing had been accomplished. "The political situation," a French Intelligence agent reported, "which was rather confused until now, is becoming clearer with the absolute victory of the extremist party of which Emir Feisal openly became the head."[7] Millerand immediately told Lloyd George that the decisions of the Syrian Congress must be considered null and void.[8] Syria, Palestine, and Mesopotamia had been taken from the Turks by the Allies. And only the Allies, not the native population, could determine the fate of the former Turkish territories.[9] Lord Curzon, British foreign secretary, was furious with France. He berated Paul Cambon, French ambassador to Great Britain, that "the future of France and Great Britain in the [Middle East] was imperilled because of the way in which the French Government, in pursuance of traditional or historical aspirations, had insisted on forcing themselves into areas where the French were not welcomed by the inhabitants." Curzon, however, promised to act "loyally" with the French in an attempt "to redeem the situation."[10] He immediately informed Feisal that at least one decision of the Syrian Congress must be rescinded: "The right of any body at Damascus to decide the future of Mesopotamia [Iraq] or Mosul is one that cannot be admitted in any circumstances." Curzon also requested that Feisal return to Europe to plead his case before the peace conference.[11] Millerand sent a similar letter to Feisal. However, there was one significant difference between the two letters: Paris refused to recognize that the Syrian Congress had the right to decide the status of Syria and Lebanon.[12] Feisal was not intimidated by either warning. He may have been encouraged by the obvious continued differences between England and France. He told France that before he could return to Europe and the peace conference, France must guarantee Arab independence in Syria, and French troops must immediately evacuate Lebanon.[13]

There was a solid basis for Feisal's excessive confidence and demands. Gouraud reported in late March that in Lebanon

our [French] prestige suffers greatly in the entire area because of a shortage of military manpower which makes us incapable of guaranteeing order. The Sherifians are taking advantage of the situation and terrorizing our followers, occupying the country, flying the flag of their new king there, and giving the people the choice between support for his party or their destruction.

And from the Syrians, Gouraud was greatly concerned:

We remain under the threat of an attack which can be launched at any time. Everywhere the political agitation caused by the proclamations of the Syrian Congress is extreme. In Syria it is no secret that every means will be used to force us to recognize the decisions of the Congress. Military preparations [in Syria] are openly being taken.[14]

Under these depressing conditions Gouraud could only advise "a wait-and-see policy, allowing us to avoid attempting a military solution to a problem which is insolvable at the present time."[15]

If Millerand intended to break the decisions of the Syrian Congress, he would need three things: British consent for military action against Feisal; reinforcements for General Gouraud; and peace in Cilicia where Mustapha Kemal and the Turkish nationalists were waging successful battles against the French, thereby encouraging the Arab nationalists to resist France and, at the same time, preventing French troops from moving southward for possible deployment against the Arab nationalists.

In the early spring of 1920 difficulties with Great Britain persisted. But they were not insurmountable. Lord Curzon notified Paris at the end of March of Britain's latest Middle Eastern strategy. He suggested that Feisal be invited to the next meeting of the peace conference, to be held at San Remo in late April. If Feisal attended the conference and fulfilled two conditions, France and England should recognize him as king of Syria. The two basic conditions were that Feisal's selection as king be "validated by a constitutional procedure" demonstrating that he was the representative of the Syrian people and that he should be permitted to make substantially different agreements with France and England concerning their respective roles in Syria and Palestine.[16]

France believed that Curzon's recommendations were predicated on the desire to assure Great Brit-

---

[6] Zeine N. Zeine, *The Struggle for Arab Independence: Western Diplomacy and the Rise and Fall of Faisal's Kingdom in Syria* (Beirut, 1960), chap. vii.

[7] Naval Intelligence memo, "Rapport hebdomadaire," Mar. 12, 1920, AAE, série: Levant S-L-C, vol. 24, fol. 29.

[8] Millerand to P. Cambon, Mar. 11, 1920, *ibid.*, vol. 25, fol. 5.

[9] Millerand to Gouraud, Mar. 13, 1920, *ibid.*, fol. 61.

[10] Curzon to Lord Derby, Mar. 13, 1920, BD, 1st series, vol. 13, no. 221, p. 228.

[11] Curzon to Allenby, quoted in P. Cambon to Millerand, Mar. 13, 1920, AAE, série: Levant S-L-C, vol. 24, fol. 55.

[12] Millerand to Gouraud, Mar. 12, 1920, *ibid.*, fol. 62.

[13] Gouraud to Millerand, Mar. 25, 1920, AMG, 6N 194.

[14] Gouraud to Millerand, Mar. 28, 1920, Archives du Ministère de la Guerre, Section Outre-Mer, Château de Vincennes, Vincennes, fonds: L'Armée du Levant, carton 3656, liasse 4.

[15] Gouraud to Millerand, Mar. 25, 1920, AAE, série: Levant S-L-C, vol. 25, fol. 193.

[16] P. Cambon to Millerand, Mar. 30, 1920, *ibid.*, fols. 263–264.

ain's supremacy in the Middle East and the belief that France possessed neither the manpower nor the will to change the recent decisions of the Syrian National Congress. Millerand, however, rejected Curzon's recommendations. France would not recognize Feisal as king, for to do so "would lead us even now to recognize a Syrian state which would include all the regions reserved under our influence and which would constitute a permanent obstacle to our policy of autonomous states." Millerand was also incensed by Curzon's implication that Great Britain's position in Palestine would be different from France's in Syria. Would a British mandate for Palestine mean direct British control of Palestine whereas a French mandate in Syria would only mean that France would serve as a rubberstamp for Feisal? Millerand wanted equality with England; that is, France should have the same role in Syria as England would have in Palestine and Mesopotamia.[17]

Millerand effectively countered Curzon's proposals. The French premier struck at one of England's most vulnerable positions: Palestine. Millerand reminded Curzon that, according to the Sykes-Picot agreement, Palestine should be placed under international jurisdiction.[18] The possibility that the status of Palestine would remain unsettled, at a time when England was beset by a cluster of colonial problems in Ireland, India, Egypt, and Mesopotamia,[19] induced Great Britain to approve formally the French mandate for Lebanon and Syria when the Allied Supreme Council met at San Remo in late April. In return, France recognized Palestine and Mesopotamia as British mandates.

The San Remo decision was important. Symbolically, it meant that France and England shared equal status in the Middle East. In practical terms, the San Remo decision meant that for the first time England would acquiesce to any action taken by France in Syria. Lord Hardinge explained England's policy:

I am afraid that it is impossible for us to interfere [in Syria]. Since grant of Mandate for Syria to French at San Remo they have possessed a prior right with reference to purely Syrian affairs which it would be neither right nor expedient for us to contest. Any attempt on our part to do so would produce greatest possible irritation here and would merely result in old game of one party being played up against other out there. French disinterest themselves altogether from Palestine and Mesopotamia, employing same argument as regards our position in those countries.[20]

Now that the argument against England had been won, Millerand could turn his full attention to Feisal. The Syrian leader had failed to attend the San Remo conference because France and England had refused to recognize Syria's independence.[21] Millerand would only guarantee Syrian independence "against all aggression coming across the [Syrian] frontiers."[22] It soon became apparent that Millerand was not referring to French aggression. In fact, Millerand had decided to subvert the Feisal-Clemenceau agreement of January 6. A week following the San Remo conference Millerand wrote to Gouraud:

I am asking you to specify . . . the course of action which would seem to you the most suitable in order to give France the role and authority which would uphold its traditions, its sacrifices, and the decisions of the Peace Conference.

The premier then explained the answer that he wanted:

The maintenance and strengthening of our traditional position can find added support through the use of new policies which recently have seen the establishment of the League of Nations and given people the right to govern themselves. By promoting the gradual development of local autonomies . . . (Lebanon, Druze, Nossayri), we can ensure under our influence various elements whose advantage you and I both appreciate.[23]

Feisal also considered the January 6 agreement to be outmoded. In early May he informed France of his basis for any further negotiations between the two countries. Syria would select her technical advisers from all countries, not just from France, and Syria's diplomatic representatives would be Arabs, not French.[24] The Syrian leader, rejecting Millerand's notion of "autonomies," told the French premier that "the Syrian people do not belong to various distinct nations but to one single nation and for a thousand years they have inhabited a single region having a common history and similar aspirations."[25]

Millerand found the situation intolerable. He was convinced that "the successive concessions which

---

[17] Quai d'Orsay memo, early Apr., 1920, *ibid.*, vol. 26, fols. 237–238; Millerand to P. Cambon, Mar. 31, 1920, *ibid.*, vol. 25, fol. 295. See also Gouraud to Millerand, Apr. 7, 1920, *ibid.*, vol. 26, fol. 69.

[18] Millerand to P. Cambon, Mar. 31, 1920, *ibid.*, vol. 25, fol. 296.

[19] P. Cambon to Millerand, Apr. 1, 1920, *ibid.*, vol. 26, fol. 3.

[20] Hardinge, permanent undersecretary of state at the Foreign Office, to Allenby, July 16, 1920, BD, 1st series, vol. 13, no. 284, p. 313.

[21] Feisal's letter to Millerand contained in Gouraud to Millerand, Apr. 3, 1920, AAE, série: Levant S-L-C, vol. 26, fols. 31–36.

[22] Millerand to P. Cambon, Apr. 5, 1920, *ibid.*, fol. 46.

[23] Millerand to Gouraud, May 4, 1920, *ibid.*, vol. 27, fols. 149, 151.

[24] General de la Panousse, chief of the French military mission in England, to Millerand, May 8, 1920, Archives du Ministère de la Guerre, Section Outre-Mer, fonds: L'Armée du Levant, carton 3649, liasse Angleterre, no. 51.

[25] Feisal's letter is contained in Gouraud to Millerand, May 19, 1920, AAE, série: Levant S-L-C, vol. 28, fol. 46.

have been made have only resulted in emboldening our enemies and compromising our positions."[26] The premier now checked with London. Curzon flashed the green light on May 18 when he told Millerand that "the French authorities must be the best judges of the military measures necessary to control the local situation, and . . . they [the French authorities] have complete authority in taking such measures."[27] The next day the French government decided that there was but one solution to the Syrian problem:

> Action against Feisal is indispensable and urgent. . . . It is extremely important that immediate decisions be taken before the attrition of the [French] troops increases to the point of necessitating an almost total replacement of our forces in Syria and also before the Sherifians become better organized. Specific political plans must be drawn up and a military plan immediately set up and put into execution.[28]

On May 22 Gouraud received his instructions and a promise that two additional divisions would be forthcoming: "Most of the manpower and material resources will be concentrated in Syria with the goal of occupying the Sherifian capital, Damascus, and the military center at Aleppo as soon as possible."[29] According to Millerand military aggression against Feisal could be justified. The premier told a hesitant Gouraud that the Sherifians had attempted

> to preempt the decisions of the peace conference by having a king of Syria proclaimed at Damascus. . . . It is obvious that the serious objections caused by such a situation cannot be prolonged and that if the Arab authorities at Damascus did not want to or could not maintain order and security, then the mandatory powers would themselves have the duty to act there for the good of the people. . . .[30]

Millerand's decision was not unanimously welcomed within the Quai d'Orsay. An anonymous memorandum, written in late May by perhaps Berthelot or one of the architects of the January 6 agreement, challenged Millerand's current Syrian policies. This memorandum pointed out that France had three choices in Syria. First, France could assume a defensive position in Cilicia while more than 60,000 French troops marched on Damascus. Thereafter, France would be bogged down for decades in an attempt to pacify the country. French public opinion, it was thought, would never tolerate the human and monetary costs of a military occupation of Syria. Secondly, France could have a mandate in Lebanon but completely abandon any role in Syria. French public opinion would never accept this solution, for it would appear to be a humiliating defeat. Thirdly, France could once again attempt to negotiate an agreement with Feisal wherein France would have the mandate for Syria. France would supply some of the technical advisers—but nothing more. It was argued that the third choice, a resurrection of the January 6 accord, was the best one for France because it would assure France's prestige at a nominal price.[31] The advice, however, was too little, too late. Millerand had decided to resort to military means to solve the Syrian impasse while Feisal was determined to prevent France from having a foothold in Syria.[32]

Meanwhile, Gouraud prepared "decisive action" against Feisal.[33] And the colonialists at the Quai d'Orsay, including Millerand, were making plans for a Syria without Feisal. The Quai d'Orsay's blueprint for "French" Syria was wildly optimistic. French economic interests would have a bonanza. Once Feisal had been overthrown, France confidently expected to rule Syria as easily as it had ruled the natives in prewar Africa. France would respect local customs and traditions. A handful of Arab collaborators could be found to serve on the various local governments of a splintered Syrian state. A modicum of Arab self-determination at the local level would be adequate to "avoid seeing the most westernized and hence the most dangerous elements turn to a nationalist agitation. . . ." The Syrians would quickly learn to appreciate French rule:

> It would be advantageous to allow these people who now would not ask for our advice to experience briefly . . . their incapacity at governing themselves; our intervention later would only be more appreciated for it.
> The collaboration of our administrative and technical advisers must be appreciated by the people, not as a fact to which they must be submitted, but as a favor which is accorded them.[34]

With such enticing prospects it was not surprising that throughout the late spring and early summer of 1920 Millerand exhorted Gouraud to prepare military action against Syria. Millerand believed that an opportunity to precipitate a crisis with Feisal was fast approaching. A truce had been arranged with Kemal and the Turkish nationalists on June 1. Furthermore, the Greek invasion of western Turkey would soon divert Turkish troops from Cilicia. French troops could now be pulled out of Cilicia and con-

---

[26] Millerand to Gouraud, May 11, 1920, *ibid.*, vol. 27, fol. 240.
[27] Curzon to Millerand, May 18, 1920, *ibid.*, vol. 28, fol. 35.
[28] "Proposition d'une réunion de conférence pour rédaction d'instructions au général Gouraud," May 19, 1920, *ibid.*, fols. 76–77.
[29] Memo by Millerand, "Projet . . . instructions générales préparées par le ministre des affaires étrangères pour le général Gouraud," May 22, 1920, *ibid.*, fol. 167.
[30] Millerand to Gouraud, May 26, 1920, *ibid.*, fol. 234.

[31] Quai d'Orsay memo, "Note sur la politique française en Syrie-Cilicie," May 27, 1920, *ibid.*, fols. 273–274.
[32] Feisal's letter to Millerand in Gouraud to Millerand, June 10, 1920, *ibid.*, vol. 29, fol. 234.
[33] Gouraud to Millerand, June 1, 1920, *ibid.*, fol. 88.
[34] Quai d'Orsay memo, May 30, 1920, *ibid.*, fols. 27–28.

centrated at Beirut for deployment in Syria.[35]

On previous occasions Millerand had requested of Feisal that France be permitted to use Syrian railways in order to transport troops and supplies to Cilicia. Feisal had rejected these requests because France had not recognized the legitimacy of the Syrian National Congress. Millerand now instructed Gouraud to tell Feisal in the form of an ultimatum that French troops would occupy the Aleppo-Rayek railroad.[36] Millerand hoped that Feisal would resist this demand. The result would be the "disappearance of the Sherifians."[37]

On July 14 Gouraud sent an ultimatum to Feisal. The ultimatum criticized the Syrian government for tolerating guerrilla attacks against French troops, not accepting the French mandate, and for ruling in defiance of the peace conference. The ultimatum demanded French control of the Rayek-Aleppo railroad, the repeal of the Syrian conscription law, the acceptance of the French mandate, and the punishment of those who were the "most violent enemies of France." Feisal was given until July 18 to accept the ultimatum. Feisal immediately asked for a two-day extension. Gouraud agreed and set midnight of July 20 as the new deadline.[38]

The granting of a two-day extension upset Millerand. He warned Gouraud of Feisal's duplicity:

It is possible that Feisal, encouraged by foreign agents desirous of not allowing us to rid ourselves of the Sherifian difficulty, may pretend to give in. In this case he will try to negotiate and to obtain terms which would bind us. I bring to your attention in this respect that this ultimatum, while demanding the acceptance of the mandate, can offer the Emir an opportunity to try to have himself recognized [as ruler of Syria]. . . .[39]

Feisal accepted the ultimatum. But the telegram accepting the conditions of the ultimatum arrived one day late, on July 21; the delay had been due to a breakdown of the telegraph lines. Nevertheless, Gouraud had ordered French troops into Syria. Millerand was greatly concerned that Feisal would survive. The premier told Gouraud on July 21:

It is essential in your relations with Emir Feisal that you follow the instructions and the full spirit of my telegrams according to which you must no longer engage in any discussion with the Emir nor negotiate as one power to another. It is necessary . . . to avoid at all costs giving the Emir an opportunity of winning when our material resources have now reached a maximum. . . .

In this connection I am afraid that the Emir's acceptance of the terms that you have posed by your ultimatum and which are a bare minimum prevent us from freeing ourselves of the Emir although we are free to do so. It is advisable to make the application of your terms so strict that the Emir will find himself bound hand and foot and from the outset will be completely powerless.[40]

Gouraud was in a bind. French troops were moving towards Damascus; yet, Feisal was fulfilling the terms of the ultimatum. Gouraud was concerned that to continue the offensive under these conditions put into question France's honor and sense of "fair play."[41] At the same time, Millerand was demanding Feisal's removal as ruler of Syria. Gouraud attempted to satisfy both Millerand and his own sense of military honor. On July 22 Gouraud stopped the unopposed French march on Damascus and gave Feisal a twenty-four-hour ultimatum, one with new conditions. This latest ultimatum explicitly demanded that France be given complete control of Syria's military, political, administrative, financial, educational, and judicial systems.[42]

Millerand was enraged by the stopping of the offensive. The premier criticized Gouraud's pangs of consciousness. Feisal and his advisers had, after all, never demonstrated "fair play."[43] Millerand criticized Gouraud's caution:

So as not to fall back into the previous situation, it is now necessary to continue to take, and without lending yourself to the Sherifians' game to gain time, all steps necessary for your safety and for the total execution of the mandate.[44]

Millerand need not have been concerned. Feisal refused Gouraud's latest ultimatum. Gouraud resumed his march on Damascus in the morning of July 24. The Sherifians put up a "strong resistance." The battle of Maysalun, a few miles west of Damascus, was over in eight hours. The French, losing two hundred men, used tanks, airplanes, and heavy artillery to overwhelm the Arabs. French troops entered Damascus unopposed. The next day Feisal fled and France created a new Syrian government comprised of carefully selected collaborators.[45]

---

[35] Millerand to Gouraud, June 13, 15, 26, 1920, *ibid.*, vol. 30, fols. 67, 79, 178–179.

[36] Millerand to Gouraud, June 1, 1920, *ibid.*, vol. 29, fol. 101.

[37] Millerand to Gouraud, June 15, 1920, *ibid.*, vol. 30, fols. 79–80.

[38] Gouraud's letter is in Sati Al Husri, *The Day of Maysalūn* (Washington, D.C., 1966), pp. 150–155; see also pp. 60–63.

[39] Millerand to Gouraud, July 18, 1920, AAE, série: Levant S-L-C, vol. 31, fol. 26. See also Millerand to Gouraud, July 18, 1920, *ibid.*, fol. 70.

[40] Millerand to Gouraud, July 21, 1920, *ibid.*, fol. 99.

[41] See the Army of the Levant report, "Rapport hebdomadaire," July 27, 1920, AMG, 6N 189, dossier: AFL.

[42] A copy of the ultimatum can be found in Husri, 1966: pp. 69–70. See also Gouraud to Millerand, July 22, 1920, AMG, 6N 194.

[43] Millerand to Gouraud, July 24, 1920, AAE, série: Levant S-L-C, vol. 31, fol. 164.

[44] Millerand to Gouraud, July 23, 1920, *ibid.*, fol. 117. See also Millerand to Gouraud, July 24, 1920, *ibid.*, fol. 164.

[45] Army of the Levant report, "Rapport hebdomadaire," July 27, 1920, AMG, 6N 189, dossier: AFL. For the battle of Maysalun and the events leading up to it, see General Mariano Goybet, "Le Combat de Khan Meiseloun 24 juillet 1920," *Revue des troupes du Levant* **2**, 5 (1937): pp. 7–38.

France now had the Syrian as well as Lebanese mandates. Millerand immediately sent Gouraud a memorandum in which the premier sketched his conception of what France's role in Syria should be. The document is revealing not only because it set France's initial policy in Syria, but because it set the tone for French policy in Syria for the next twenty-five years. In so doing, the document helps to explain why France encountered guerrilla warfare, sabotage, general strikes, and full-scale warfare in Syria until forced to leave during World War II.

Theoretically, France's role as a mandatory was to have guided Syria and Lebanon until they could rule themselves. France was to have served as a trustee for the League of Nations. However, as Millerand made clear, reality was different from theory. There was nothing altruistic about France's desire to have a mandate in the Middle East:

> In assuming the mandate in Syria, France has not attempted to create a new colony but to maintain a century-old situation necessary for her place in the Mediterranean; she [France] wishes to ensure her influence there. . . .

The first thing that Millerand ordered Gouraud to do was to break Syria into several political units. Millerand thought that it would be easier to rule a divided nation. Superimposed upon this fragmented country, Millerand placed a huge French bureaucracy. French officialdom, led by the high commissioner, was to direct all aspects of Syrian and Lebanese life. The bureaucracy was to have a humanitarian purpose: "French supervision must be especially responsive to the safety of people and property, with an eye to the economic development of the country, and the introduction of civic morality and self-respect which until now has been nonexistent." The police should be "fair." The tax structure should be impartial and equitable. The protection of minorities was deemed the "fundamental job of the mandatory." By this Millerand meant the Christians, the only ones who actively supported the French mandate. Lebanon was favored at the expense of Moslem Syria. A few days after Feisal's defeat, Gouraud annexed the Bekaa region to Lebanon, thereby creating an enlarged Lebanon.

The French bureaucracy could give the Syrians greater "efficiency" in administering the educational, legal, financial, and health services. But the basic purpose of the French bureaucracy in Syria was the same as that of the French colonial administration during the Ancien Régime, Napoleonic era, and the prewar Third Republic: control in the form of paternal authoritarianism. Millerand did not believe that the Arabs should participate in the political decisions affecting their lives. Wilsonian idealism and the notion of national self-determination were rejected:

> The concept of a direct parliamentary organization corresponds in no way to the present state of political education of the country. The goal of the mandatory power is to look upon the situation in Syria in a realistic way, conforming to the interests of the majority of the people and not of a few politically oriented groups.[46]

"With our force and our generosity," Gouraud optimistically observed, "a French peace—finer than the *pax romana*—will reign over the vast Bedouin territory up to the Euphrates River."[47] Gouraud and Millerand underestimated the possibility that the Arabs, whether westernized Damascenes or feudal Druze, did not want to be ruled by France. The usually realistic *Correspondance d'Orient* blithely and blindly dismissed the possibility that Arab discontent could disrupt "la paix française":

> French influence will be exercised in the mildest way—through advice and inspiration. . . . In this way we shall avoid the frustrations of the English in Mesopotamia. . . . The frustrations of our Allies have been provoked, not by the opposition of nationalism, but by the protest against an . . . administration completely ignorant of native customs.
> We have enough experience with the Moslems . . . to avoid these errors. Freed from a foreign body [Feisal and Sherifians] which was the sole cause of friction, Franco-Syrian collaboration will be fruitful. . . . Governed well, Syria will be for France what she formerly was for Rome.[48]

Much of liberal republican France concurred. Syria and all of France's colonies were expected to serve postwar France by supplying manpower for the depleted French armies, by supplying raw materials for France's devastated heavy industry, by serving as a market for French manufactured goods, and by becoming the exclusive domain of French finance. In return, Syria would receive the benefits of French civilization such as a higher material standard of living, law and order, schools, and hospitals.[49] Unfortunately, France would spend much of the interwar period discovering that only superior force, whether bureaucratic or military, could maintain this kind of arrangement.

CONCLUSION

Many factors explain France's need to take a commanding position in the Middle East during World War I and the peace conference: cultural and religious traditions; imperial competition with England; spoils, in the form of prestige and opportunity for economic exploitation, for a wartime victor; the

---

[46] Millerand to Gouraud, Aug. 6, 1920, AAE, série: Levant S-L-C, vol. 32, fols. 55–59.

[47] General Henri Gouraud, "La France en Syrie," *Revue de France*, Apr. 1, 1922: p. 515.

[48] Saint-Brice, "La Syrie sauvée," *Correspondance d'Orient*, nos. 243–244 (Aug. 15–30, 1915): p. 61.

[49] Sarraut, 1923: chaps. i–iii; Raoul Girardet, *L'Idée coloniale en France de 1871 à 1962* (Paris, 1972), chap. vi.

relationship between the Middle East and France's Arab possessions in North Africa; and the need, sharpened by the wartime sacrifices, to seek compensation for the loss of a preeminent position within the prewar Ottoman Empire.

But these reasons do not fully explain France's military conquest of Syria in July, 1920. There was nothing inevitable about the French invasion and military occupation. It is necessary to focus upon the Feisal-Clemenceau agreement of January 6, 1920. The agreement was a compromise. France, without a military occupation, would have been recognized as the dominant power in Syria. Yet there was a good deal of latitude for native self-rule. The agreement was reached only after England's attempt to keep France out of Syria had failed, only after France's attempt to gain complete control of Syria had failed, and only after Feisal's attempts to gain complete independence had failed.

The January 6 agreement might have succeeded had it been arranged a year earlier in Paris when Feisal still had control over the Arab nationalists and Clemenceau's prestige was at its height. But both leaders were shortsighted. In the spring of 1919 Clemenceau made unrealistic demands. And so did Feisal, who found Great Britain to be a convenient shield against French pretensions. By January, 1920, new factors had emerged to destroy the Feisal-Clemenceau agreement. Arab nationalists would not accept Feisal's attempts to promote the French mandate, and Millerand replaced Clemenceau as premier. Millerand was determined to assert French military superiority against the "winds of change." In the short term Millerand's policy was successful, and the Arab nationalists were temporarily curbed. But in the long run the twenty-five-year French experience as a mandatory proved to be wasteful, debilitating, and humiliating—for the French and the Arabs.

APPENDIX

1. THE ANGLO–FRENCH AGREEMENT OF 1916

(Lord Grey to Paul Cambon, May 16, 1916)
BD, 1st series, vol. 4: pp. 245–247)

I have the honour to inform Your Excellency in reply that . . . they [British government] are ready to accept the arrangement now arrived at, provided that the co-operation of the Arabs is secured, and that the Arabs fulfill the conditions and obtain the towns of Homs, Hama, Damascus, and Aleppo.

It is accordingly understood between the French and British Governments:

1. That France and Great Britain are prepared to recognize and protect an independent Arab State or a Confederation of Arab States in the areas (A) and (B) marked on the annexed map, under the suzerainty of an Arab chief. That in area (A) France, and in area (B) Great Britain, shall have priority of right of enterprise and local loans. That in area (A) France, and in area (B) Great Britain, shall alone supply advisers or foreign functionaries at the request of the Arab State or Confederation of Arab States.

2. That in the blue area France, and in the red area Great Britain, shall be allowed to establish such direct or indirect administration or control as they desire and as they may think fit to arrange with the Arab State or Confederation of Arab States.

3. That in the brown area [Palestine] there shall be established an international administration, the form of which is to be decided upon after consultation with Russia, and subsequently in consultation with the other Allies, and the representatives of the Shereef of Mecca.

4. That Great Britain be accorded (1) the ports of Haifa and Acre; (2) guarantee of a given supply of water from the Tigris and Euphrates in area (A) for area (B). His Majesty's Government, on their part, undertake that they will at no time enter into negotiations for the cession of Cyprus to any third Power without the previous consent of the French Government.

5. That Alexandretta shall be a free port as regards the trade of the British Empire, and that there shall be no discrimination in port charges or facilities as regards British shipping and British goods; that there shall be freedom of transit for British goods through Alexandretta and by railway through the blue area, whether those goods are intended for or originate in the red area, or (B) area, or area (A); and there shall be no discrimination, direct or indirect, against British goods on any railway or against British goods or ships at any port serving the areas mentioned.

That Haifa shall be a free port as regards the trade of France, her dominions and protectorates, and there shall be no discrimination in port charges or facilities as regards French shipping and French goods. There shall be freedom of transit for French goods through Haifa and by the British railway through the brown area, whether these goods are intended for or originate in the blue area, area (A), or area (B), and there shall be no discrimination, direct or indirect, against French goods on any railway, or against French goods or ships at any port serving the areas mentioned.

6. That in area (A) the Bagdad Railway shall not be extended southwards beyond Mosul, and in area (B) northwards beyond Samarra, until a rail-

way connecting Bagdad with Aleppo via the Euphrates Valley has been completed, and then only with the concurrence of the two Governments.

7. That Great Britain has the right to build, administer, and be sole owner of a railway connecting Haifa with area (B), and shall have a perpetual right to transport troops along such a line at all times.

It is to be understood by both Governments that this railway is to facilitate the connection of Bagdad with Haifa by rail, and it is further understood that, if the engineering difficulties and expense entailed by keeping this connecting line in the brown area only make the project unfeasible, that the French Government shall be prepared to consider that the line in question may also traverse the polygon Banias-Keis Marib-Salkhad Tell Otsda-Mesmie before reaching area (B).

8. For a period of twenty years the existing Turkish customs tariff shall remain in force throughout the whole of the blue and red areas, as well as in areas (A) and (B), and no increase in the rates of duty or conversion from *ad valorem* to specific rates shall be made except by agreement between the two powers.

There shall be no interior customs barriers between any of the above-mentioned areas. The customs duties leviable on goods destined for the interior shall be collected at the port of entry and handed over to the administration of the area of destination.

9. It shall be agreed that the French Government will at no time enter into any negotiations for the cession of their rights and will not cede such rights in the blue area to any third Power, except the Arab State or Confederation of Arab States, without the previous agreement of His Majesty's Government, who, on their part, will give a similar undertaking to the French Government regarding the red area.

10. The British and French Governments, as the protectors of the Arab State, shall agree that they will not themselves acquire and will not consent to a third Power acquiring territorial possessions in the Arabian peninsula, nor consent to a third Power installing a naval base either on the east coast, or on the islands, of the Red Sea. This, however, shall not prevent such adjustment of the Aden frontier as may be necessary in consequence of recent Turkish aggression.

11. The negotiations with the Arabs as to boundaries of the Arab State or Confederation of Arab States shall be continued through the same channel as heretofore on behalf of the two Powers.

12. It is agreed that measures to control the importation of arms into the Arab territories will be considered by the two Governments. . . .

2. THE PROVISIONAL AGREEMENT OF JANUARY 6, 1920

(AAE, série: Levant, 1918–1929, Arabie, vol. 8, fols. 83–86)

The government of the French republic, basing itself, on one hand, upon the Anglo-French declaration of November 9, 1918, and, on the other hand, upon the general principles of the freedom of peoples and of the friendly collaboration proclaimed by the Peace Conference, affirms its recognition of the right of the Arabic-speaking peoples of all faiths living on Syrian land to unite and govern themselves as an independent nation.

His Royal Highness, Emir Feisal, acknowledges that, because of the chaos resulting from Turkish oppression and hardships endured during the war, it is in the interest of the Syrian peoples to ask for the advice and assistance of a great power to effect their unity and organize the administration of the nation. This advice and assistance will be recorded by the League of Nations when it is finally realized.

In the name of the Syrian people he is appealing to France to accomplish this mission.

I

The French government promises to lend its assistance to Syria, to guarantee her independence against any infringement of her frontiers as recognized by the Peace Conference.

Concerning the determination of these frontiers, the French government will endeavor to obtain every equitable settlement from the ethnical, linguistic, and geographical point of view.

II

His Royal Highness, Emir Feisal, promises to ask the government of the French republic and only this government for the counsellors, instructors, and technical advisers necessary to organize the civil and military administrations. These advisers and technicians will be placed at the disposition of the Syrian government. Their investiture and powers of authority will be determined by common consent of the two governments in an agreement specifying the duration and obligations of their mission.

The government of the Republic and his Royal Highness, Emir Feisal, agree to establish a constitutional regime in Syria, which, assuring the political rights of the people and upholding freedoms previously obtained and in conformity to their wishes, requires the establishment of a government responsible to the Parliament.

In order to permit the financial reorganization which is the basis of the whole administration of the new state, the financial adviser will participate in the preparation of the budget of money spent and money received, and he will be notified of all expenses budgeted by the various departments. He will audit the part of the Ottoman public debt pertaining to Syria and will be entrusted with questions concerning the application of the financial clauses of the peace treaty with Turkey to Syria.

The adviser of Public Works will have the railroads under his jurisdiction. The special status of the Hejaz railroad will be respected. Any arrangement changing the free economic functioning of the railroads leading to Damascus for the benefit of a third party will be null and void.

As soon as the conclusion of the present agreement is reached, the French government will lend its assistance for the organization of the gendarmerie, police, and army.

His Royal Highness, Emir Feisal, acknowledges the top priority right of the French government in the undertakings and loans necessary for the good of the country, except in opposition to nationals who are acting for themselves and not lending their name to foreign capital.

III

The Syrian state will be represented abroad and the French government will lend its good offices to facilitate her entry into the League of Nations.

His Royal Highness, Emir Feisal, will maintain a diplomatic delegate with the French government in Paris. He will entrust France's diplomatic and consular representatives abroad with representing Syria's foreign interests.

IV

His Royal Highness recognizes the independence and integrity of Lebanon under the French mandate. The boundaries [of Lebanon] will be determined by the Peace Conference, taking into account the rights, interests, and wishes of the people.

V

Arabic will be recognized as the official and administrative language and will be used in the schools. The study of the French language will be required in the schools.

VI

Damascus will be the capital and residence of the Syrian Chief of State. The High Commissioner representing France will have his usual residence at Aleppo, thus remaining near Cilicia, a border zone, where [French] security forces will normally be concentrated. Their [French security forces] entry into Syria will be accomplished upon the request of the head of the Syrian state in agreement with the French High Commissioner.

BIBLIOGRAPHY

MANUSCRIPT AND ARCHIVAL SOURCES

France

Paris

Archives du Ministère des Affaires Etrangères, Quai d'Orsay.
    Série: Guerre 1914–1918.
        A Paix.
        Levant, 1918–1929.
        Papiers d'Agents.
Bibliothèque de l'Institut de France.
    Pichon, Stéphen. Correspondance.

Vincennes

Archives Centrales de la Marine, Château de Vincennes.
    Série: Ea
          S
Archives du Ministère de la Guerre, Service Historique, Château de Vincennes.
    Fonds: 4N (Conseil Supérieur de Guerre)
           5N (Cabinet du Ministre)
           6N (Particuliers)
           7N (E.M.A.)
Archives du Ministère de la Guerre, Section Outre-Mer, Château de Vincennes.
    Fonds: L'Armée du Levant.
Bibliothèque Historique des Archives Centrales de la Marine, Château de Vincennes.
    Guichard, Lieutenant de Vaisseau Louis. n.d. "Les Forces navales françaises en Syrie, Egypte, Mer Rouge, 1914–1918."
    This volume is excellent because it contains detailed correspondence between the minister of the navy and the naval commanders.

Great Britain

London

Public Record Office.
    Cabinet Office Papers.
        Cabs. 1, 2, 4, 15, 17, 21, 22, 23, 24, 27, 28, 42.
    Foreign Office Papers.
        F.O. 371: Foreign Office Correspondence.
        F.O. 608: Peace Conference.
        F.O. 800: Private Papers.
        F.O. 882: Arab Bureau Papers.
    War Office Papers.
        W.O. 106: Military Operations and Intelligence.
House of Lords Record Office.
    Lloyd George, David. Papers.
India Office and Records.
    Curzon, Lord. Papers.

GOVERNMENT DOCUMENTS AND OFFICIAL HISTORIES

France

Assemblée Nationale. *Journal officiel, Chambre des Députés, Débats parlementaires* (1912–1920).
———. *Journal officiel, Sénat, Débats parlementaires* (1912–1920).
Ministère de la Guerre, Etat-Major de l'Armée, Service Historique. 1923–1939. *Les Armées françaises dans la grande guerre* (68 v., Paris, Imprimerie Nationale).

Great Britain

Committee of Imperial Defence, Historical Section. 1930. *History of the Great War Based on Official Documents:*

Military Operations: Egypt and Palestine From June 1917 to the End of the War, edited by Cyril Falls and A. F. Becke (2 v., London, H. M. Stationery Office).

Foreign Office, Historical Section. 1947–1976. *Documents on British Foreign Policy, 1919–1939*, 1st series (20 v., London, H. M. Stationery Office). Vol. 4 (1952), edited by E. L. Woodward and Rohan Butler; vols. 7, 8 (1958), and 13 (1963), edited by Rohan Butler and J. P. T. Bury.

United States

Department of State. 1942–1947. *Papers Relating to the Foreign Relations of the United States, 1919: The Paris Peace Conference* (13 v., Washington, D.C., U.S. Government Printing Office).

Russia

Ministry of Foreign Affairs. 1928. *Documents diplomatiques secrets russes, 1914–1917: d'après les Archives du Ministère des Affaires Etrangères à Petrograd* (translated by J. Polonsky, Paris, Payot).

NEWSPAPERS AND JOURNALS

L'Action française
L'Asie française
Correspondance d'Orient
La Croix
L'Ere nouvelle
Le Figaro
L'Humanité
New York Times
Le Temps
Times (London)

MEMOIRS AND CONTEMPORARY SOURCES

ANON. 1921. "L'Organisation de la Syrie sous le mandat français." *Revue des deux mondes*, December 1, 1921, **6**: pp. 633–663.

AULNEAU, J. 1914. "La Question syrienne." *Revue politique et parlementaire* **81**: pp. 81–99.

BRÉMOND, GENERAL EDOUARD. 1931. *Le Hedjaz dans la guerre mondiale* (Paris, Payot).

CALLWELL, MAJOR GENERAL SIR C. E. 1927. *Field Marshall Sir Henry Wilson* (2 v., London, Cassell & Co.).

CATROUX, GEORGES. 1958. *Deux Missions en Moyen-Orient* (Paris, Plon).

CLEMENCEAU, GEORGES. 1930. *Grandeur and Misery of Victory* (New York, Harcourt, Brace & Co.).

DARTIGE DU FOURNET, LOUIS. 1920. *Souvenirs de guerre d'un amiral, 1914–1916* (Paris, Plon).

FABRE-LUCE, ALFRED. 1922. *La Crise des alliances: Essai sur les relations franco-britanniques depuis la signature de la paix (1919–1922)* (Paris, Bernard Grasset).

FLANDIN, ETIENNE. 1915. "Nos droits en Syrie et en Palestine." *La Revue hebdomadaire* **4**: pp. 17–32.

GAUTHEROT, GUSTAVE. 1920. *La France en Syrie et en Cilicie* (Courbevoie [Seine], Librairie indépendante).

GONTAUT-BIRON, COMTE ROGER DE. 1922. *Comment la France s'est installée en Syrie, 1918–1919* (Paris, Plon).

GOURAUD, GENERAL HENRI. 1922. "La France en Syrie." *Revue de France*, April 1, 1922: pp. 497–517.

GOYBET, GENERAL MARIANO. 1937. "Le Combat de Khan Meiseloun, 24 juillet 1920." *Revue des troupes du Levant* **2,5**: pp. 7–38.

GREY, EDWARD. 1925. *Twenty-Five Years, 1892–1916* (2 v., New York, Frederick A. Stokes).

HEADLAM-MORLEY, SIR JAMES. 1972. *A Memoir of the Paris Peace Conference 1919* (London, Methuen & Co.).

HUSRI, SATI AL. 1966. *Day of Maysalūn* (translated by Sidney Glazer, Washington, D.C., Middle East Institute).

JUNG, EUGÈNE. 1924–1925. *La Révolte arabe* (2 v., Paris, Colbert).

LARCHER, GENERAL M. 1926. *La Guerre turque dans la guerre mondiale* (Paris, Berger-Levrault).

LAWRENCE, T. E. 1975. *Seven Pillars of Wisdom* (New York, Penguin).

LENNOX, LADY ALGERNON GORDON [Blanche], ed. 1924. *The Diary of Lord Bertie of Thame, 1914–1918* (2 v., London, Hodder & Stoughton).

LLOYD GEORGE, DAVID. 1933–1937. *War Memoirs of David Lloyd George* (6 v., Boston, Little, Brown & Co.).

———. 1939. *Memoirs of the Peace Conference* (2 v., New Haven, Yale University Press).

LODER, J. DE V. 1923. *The Truth about Mesopotamia, Palestine, and Syria* (London, Allen & Unwin).

MADELIN, LOUIS. 1917. "La Syrie franque." *Revue des deux mondes*, March 1917, **2**: pp. 314–358.

MANTOUX, PAUL. 1955. *Les Délibérations du conseil des quatre: 24 mars–28 juin 1919* (2 v., Paris, Editions du centre national de la recherche scientifique).

MILLER, DAVID HUNTER. 1924. *My Diary at the Conference of Paris* (21 v., New York, Appeal Printing Company).

MORDACQ, JEAN J. 1930–1931. *Le Ministère Clemenceau: Journal d'un témoin* (4 v., Paris, Plon).

PALÉOLOGUE, MAURICE. 1923–1925. *An Ambassador's Memoirs* (translated by F. A. Holt, 3 v., 4th ed., New York, George H. Doran).

PICHON, JEAN. 1932. *Sur la route des Indes, un siècle après Bonaparte* (Paris, Société d'éditions géographiques, maritimes et coloniales).

———. 1938. *Le Partage du Proche-Orient* (Paris, J. Peyronnet).

POINCARÉ, RAYMOND. 1926–1974. *Au service de la France: Neuf années de souvenirs* (11 v., Paris, Plon).

RIDDELL, G. A. 1934. *Lord Riddell's Intimate Diary of the Peace Conference and After, 1918–1923* (New York, Reynal & Hitchcock).

SAMNÉ, GEORGE. 1921. *La Syrie* (Paris, Bossard).

SARRAUT, ALBERT. 1923. *La Mise en valeur des colonies françaises* (Paris, Payot).

———. 1931. *Grandeur et servitude coloniales* (Paris, Editions du sagittaire).

SOKOLOW, NAHUM. 1969. *History of Zionism, 1600–1918* (2 v. in 1, New York, Ktav Publishing House).

STORRS, SIR RONALD. 1937. *The Memoirs of Sir Ronald Storrs* (New York, Putnam's Sons).

TAILLANDIER, SAINT-RENÉ. 1919. "La France et la Syrie, notre œuvre dans le Levant et son avenir." *Revue des deux mondes* **49** (February 15, 1919): pp. 771–804.

TARDIEU, ANDRÉ. 1921. *The Truth about the Treaty* (Indianapolis, Bobbs-Merrill).

TEMPERLEY, H. W. V., ed. 1920–1924. *A History of the Peace Conference* (6 v., London, Frowde, Hodder & Stoughton).

TESTIS. 1921. "L'Oeuvre de la France en Syrie: le général Gouraud pacificateur." *Revue des deux mondes*, January 1, 1921, **1**: pp. 801–840.

———. 1921. "L'Oeuvre de la France en Syrie: le général Gouraud organisateur." *Revue des deux mondes*, March 1, 1921, **2**: pp. 97–136.

VINCENT, CHARLES. 1915. "La Syrie." *La Revue hebdomadaire* **5**: pp. 281–302.

WICKHAM STEED, HENRY. 1924. *Through Thirty Years, 1892–1922* (2 v., London, Heinemann).

SECONDARY WORKS

ABRAMS, L., and D. J. MILLER. 1976. "Who Were the French Colonialists? A Reassessment of the Parti-Colonial, 1890–1914." **19**, 3: pp. 685–725.

BIBLIOGRAPHY

ADELSON, ROGER. 1975. *Mark Sykes: Portrait of an Amateur* (London, Jonathan Cape).

ALDINGTON, RICHARD. 1955. *Lawrence of Arabia: A Biographical Enquiry* (London, Collins).

ANDREW, C. M., and A. S. KANYA-FORSTNER. 1974. "The French Colonial Party and French Colonial War Aims, 1914–1918." *Hist. Jour.* **17**: pp. 79–106.

ANTONIUS, GEORGE. 1938. *The Arab Awakening: The Story of the Arab National Movement* (London, Hamish Hamilton).

ARTHUR, G. C. 1932. *General Sir John Maxwell* (London, Murray).

BIANQUIS, PHILIPPE J., ed. 1934. *Eléments d'une bibliographie française de l'après-guerre pour les états sous mandat du Proche-Orient, 1919–1930* (Beirut, Imprimerie catholique).

BONNEFOUS, GEORGES, and EDOUARD BONNEFOUS. 1956–1957. *Histoire politique de la troisième république* (7 v., Paris, Presses universitaires de France).

BRUNEAU, ANDRÉ. 1932. *Traditions et politique de la France au Levant* (Paris, Félix Alcan).

BRUNSCHWIG, HENRI. 1960. *Mythes et réalités de l'impérialisme colonial français, 1871–1914* (Paris, Armand Colin).

BUSCH, BRITON COOPER. 1971. *Britain, India, and the Arabs, 1914–1921* (Berkeley, University of California Press).

CASSAR, GEORGE H. 1971. *The French and the Dardanelles: A Study in Failure in the Conduct of the War* (London, George Allen & Unwin).

CHALLENER, RICHARD D. 1953. "The French Foreign Office: The Era of Philippe Berthelot." In: *The Diplomats, 1919–1939*, edited by Gordon A. Craig and Felix Gilbert (Princeton, Princeton University Press), pp. 49–86.

CHEVALLIER, DOMINIQUE. 1960. "Lyon et la Syrie en 1919: les bases d'une intervention." *Revue historique* **224**: pp. 275–320.

CHURCHILL, RANDOLPH, and MARTIN GILBERT. 1966–1976. *Winston S. Churchill* (5 v., London, Heinemann).

DAWN, C. ERNEST. 1973. *From Ottomanism to Arabism: Essays on the Origins of Arab Nationalism* (Champaign, University of Illinois Press).

EVANS, LAURENCE. 1965. *United States Policy and the Partition of Turkey, 1914–1924* (Baltimore, Johns Hopkins Press).

FABRE-LUCE, ALFRED. 1950. "Le Colonel Laurence et la France." *Les Oeuvres libres* no. 48: pp. 129–158.

FRIEDMAN, ISAIAH. 1973. *The Question of Palestine, 1914–1918: British-Jewish-Arab Relations* (London, Routledge & Kegan Paul).

GARDNER, BRIAN. 1966. *Allenby of Arabia: Lawrence's General* (New York, Coward-McCann Inc.).

GAUVAIN, AUGUSTE. 1924. "Five Years of French Policy in the Near East." *Foreign Affairs* **3**: pp. 277–292.

GIRARDET, RAOUL. 1972. *L'Idée coloniale en France de 1871 à 1962* (Paris, La Table ronde).

GOGUEL, FRANÇOIS. 1958. *La Politique des partis sous la troisième république* (3rd ed., Paris, Editions du Seuil).

HELMREICH, PAUL. 1974. *From Paris to Sèvres: The Partition of the Ottoman Empire at the Peace Conference of 1919–1920* (Columbus, Ohio State University Press).

HOPWOOD, DEREK. 1969. *The Russian Presence in Syria and Palestine, 1843–1914* (Clarendon, Oxford University Press).

HOWARD, HARRY. 1931. *The Partition of Turkey: A Diplomatic History, 1913–1923* (Norman, University of Oklahoma Press).

———. 1963. *The King-Crane Commission: An American Inquiry in the Middle East* (Beirut, Khayat's).

JOUIN, COLONEL YVES. 1967. "Les Compagnons français de Laurence." *Revue historique de l'armée* no. 4: pp. 107–121.

KEDOURIE, ELIE. 1956. *England and the Middle East: The Destruction of the Ottoman Empire, 1914–1921* (London, Bowes & Bowes).

———. 1970. *The Chatham House Version and Other Middle-Eastern Studies* (New York, Praeger).

———. 1976. *In the Anglo-Arab Labyrinth: The McMahon-Husayn Correspondence and Its Interpretations, 1914–1939* (Cambridge, Cambridge University Press).

KIRKBRIDE, SIR ALEC. 1971. *An Awakening: The Arab Campaign 1917–18* (Tavistock, England, University Press of Arabia).

LONGRIGG, STEPHEN HEMSLEY. 1958. *Syria and Lebanon under the French Mandate* (London, Oxford University Press).

LYAUTEY, PIERRE. 1949. *Gouraud* (Paris, René Julliard).

MACK, JOHN E. 1976. *A Prince of Our Disorder: The Life of T. E. Lawrence* (London, Weidenfeld & Nicolson).

MAYER, ARNO J. 1959. *Political Origins of the New Diplomacy, 1917–1918* (New Haven, Yale University Press).

———. 1967. *Politics and Diplomacy of Peacemaking: Containment and Counterrevolution at Versailles, 1918–1919* (New York, Alfred Knopf).

MILLER, D. H. 1928. "Origins of the Mandate System." *Foreign Affairs* **6**: pp. 277–289.

MINERBI, SERGIO I. 1970. *L'Italie et la Palestine, 1914–1920* (Paris, Presses universitaires de France).

MIQUEL, PIERRE. 1972. *La Paix de Versailles et l'opinion publique française* (Paris, Flammarion).

MONNERVILLE, GASTON. 1968. *Clemenceau* (Paris, Fayard).

MORSEY, KONRAD. 1976. *T. E. Lawrence und der arabische Aufstand 1916/18* (Osnabrück, Germany, Biblio).

NEVAKIVI, JUKKA. 1969. *Britain, France and the Arab Middle East, 1914–1920* (London, The Athlone Press).

NICOLSON, HAROLD. 1934. *Curzon: The Last Phase, 1919–1925* (New York, Houghton Mifflin).

OWENS, FRANK. 1954. *Tempestuous Journey—Lloyd George: His Life and Times* (London, Hutchinson & Co.).

PINGAUD, ALBERT. 1939. "Le Partage de l'Asie-Mineure pendant la grande guerre, 1915–1917." *Revue d'histoire de la guerre mondiale* **17**, 2: pp. 97–125.

PORATH, Y. 1974. *The Emergence of the Palestinian-Arab National Movement, 1918–1929* (London, Frank Cass).

ROEDERER, CARLE and PAUL. 1917. *La Syrie et la France* (Paris, Berger-Levrault).

RONALDSHAY, EARL OF. 1928. *The Life of Lord Curzon* (3 v., London, Ernest Benn).

ROTHWELL, V. H. 1971. *British War Aims and Peace Diplomacy, 1914–1918* (Oxford, Clarendon Press).

SACHAR, HOWARD. 1969. *The Emergence of the Middle East, 1914–1924* (New York, Alfred Knopf).

SADAKA, NAGIB. 1941. *La Question syrienne pendant la guerre de 1914* (Paris, Larose).

SHORROCK, WILLIAM I. 1976. *French Imperialism in the Middle East: The Failure of Policy in Syria and Lebanon, 1900–1914* (Madison, University of Wisconsin Press).

SMITH, C. JAY, JR. 1956. *The Russian Struggle for Power, 1914–1917: A Study of Russian Foreign Policy During the First World War* (New York, Philosophical Library).

SPAGNOLO, JOHN P. 1964. "French Influence in Syria Prior to World War I: The Functional Weakness of Imperialism." *Middle East Jour.* **23**: pp. 45–61.

———. 1974. "The Definition of a Style of Imperialism: The Internal Politics of the French Educational Investment in Ottoman Beirut." *French Hist. Studies* **8**: pp. 563–584.

STEIN, LEONARD. 1961. *The Balfour Declaration* (New York, Simon & Schuster).

SUAREZ, GEORGES. 1938–1941. *Briand: Sa vie—son œuvre avec son journal et de nombreux documents inédits* (6 v., Paris, Plon).

TIBAWI, A. L. 1966. "Syria in the McMahon Correspondence: Fresh Evidence from the British Foreign Office Records." *Middle East Forum* **42**, 4: pp. 5–31.

———. 1967. "Syria in Wartime Agreements and Disagreements: Fresh Evidence from the British Foreign Office Records." *Middle East Forum* **43**, 2–3: pp. 77–109.

———. 1969. *A Modern History of Syria Including Lebanon and Palestine* (London, St. Martin's Press).

THORNTON, A. P. 1968. *The Imperial Idea and Its Enemies: A Study in British Power* (Garden City, Doubleday).

WALWORTH, ARTHUR. 1958. *Woodrow Wilson* (2 v., New York, Longmans, Green & Co.).

WATSON, DAVID ROBIN. 1974. *Georges Clemenceau: A Political Biography* (London, Eyre Methuen).

WORMSER, GEORGES. 1961. *La République de Clemenceau* (Paris, Presses universitaires de France).

ZEINE, ZEINE N. 1958. *Arab-Turkish Relations and the Emergence of Arab Nationalism* (Beirut, Khayat's).

———. 1960. *The Struggle for Arab Independence: Western Diplomacy and the Rise and Fall of Faisal's Kingdom in Syria* (Beirut, Constable & Co. Ltd.).

INDEX

Abdullah, 22, 38

Action française, L', 32 n

Akaba, 7; Feisal's victory at, 19

Allenby, Edmund, 19, 20, 22, 30; curtails French influence in Syria, 21; supports Feisal at Paris Peace Conference, 28

Anglo-French Agreement of 1916. *See* Sykes-Picot agreement

Arab Revolt: reasons for, 15; reasons for French support, 15; Briand's belief that it would fail, 16; and Feisal, 19; and Feisal's entry into Damascus, 21; of little military help to the British, 22

Asie française, L', 32

Augagneur, Victor, 10; and concern about wartime British intentions in the Middle East, 6

Bagdad Railway, 5, 6

Balfour, Arthur: repudiates Sykes-Picot agreement, 21–23; claims that McMahon had promised independence to Syria, 23; and clashing Anglo-French colonial interests, 33

Balfour Declaration: and France, 25–26

Barrère, Camille, 33

Basch, Victor, 24

Berthelot, Philippe, 10, 34, 36, 40

Brémond, Edouard, 15, 16, 18, 19 n

Briand, Aristide: and the 1916 French-British (Sykes-Picot) agreement, 10–14; formulates France's Middle Eastern policies in 1915, 10, 11; concerned about British intentions in the Middle East, 12–13; and the Italian and Russian response to the Sykes-Picot agreement, 13–15; considered Sykes-Picot agreement as cornerstone of French Middle Eastern policy, 14; supports 1916 Arab Revolt, 15–16; skeptical about Arab success, 16; rejects Syrian offensive, 20; and Zionists, 24–25

Caix, Robert de, 10; shapes French policies at Paris Peace Conference, 29, 30; opposes Feisal-Clemenceau provisional agreement of January 6, 1920, 36

Cambon, Jules: recognizes the Zionist program, 25

Cambon, Paul, 10, 21, 38; skeptical of Arab rebellion against Turks, 16; and mandate for Syria, 27

Cecil, Robert: warns France, 19; seeks British control of Middle East, 22; maintains that England under no legal obligation to Arabs, 28

Churchill, Winston: and the proposed British landing at Alexandretta, 6

Clayton, Gilbert, 14, 18, 21, 31

Clemenceau, Georges, 10, 19, 20, 21, 26, 43; meets Lloyd George in London, 1918, 23; seeks French mandate for Syria and Lebanon, 27; negotiates with Feisal at Paris Peace Conference, 29–30; conflict with Great Britian at Paris Peace Conference, 28, 31–32; warns Lloyd George, 32; and the deteriorating British-French relations, 33; and the Sykes-Picot agreement, 34; undertakes a new Syrian policy, 34–37

Clerk, George: recognizes British predicament, 8

Constantine, King of Greece, 15

Correspondance d'Orient, 27, 32, 42

Croix, La, 32

Curzon, Lord: disagrees with France on Syrian problem, 38–39; agrees to French policy, 40

Damascus, 8, 28; needed by France, 6, 27; repercussions of allowing Feisal to capture, 21; nationalist agitation, 36, 37; French entered, 41

Defrance, Jules-Albert, 10, 16

Delcassé, Théophile: opposes British plans for postwar Middle East, 8

Derby, Lord, 23

Faruqi, Sherif Al-, 11

Fashoda, 19

Feisal, Emir, 19, 20, 24, 26, 27, 34, 40, 42, 43; supported by British at France's expense, 21–23, 28; seeks Syrian independence at Paris Peace Conference, 28; negotiations with France at Peace Conference, 28–31; unrealistic demands, 31; reaches a provisional agreement with Clemenceau, 35–37; recognizes dangers to the January 6, 1920, provisional agreement, 36; buffeted by Arab nationalists, 37; opposes French mandate for Syria, 38, 39; and the French ultimatums, 41

Fleuriau, Joseph de, 33

French policies in Middle East: pre-World War I concerns, 5; and Viviani government (1914–1915), 5–6, 8; reasons for France to maintain a predominant position in Middle East, 5, 6, 10, 15, 27, 32, 36, 40, 41; opposed by Great Britian, 5, 7, 9, 14, 18–19, 21–23, 28, 31–32, 33, 38–39; and Briand government (1915–1917), 10, 11, 14, 15–16; and Ribot government (1917), 16–19; and Clemenceau government (1917–1918), 19–20; Clemenceau on the eve of the Paris Peace Conference, 26; Clemenceau accepts the mandate principle, 26–27; Clemenceau at the Paris Peace Conference (1919), 26–32; Clemenceau presents a different Syrian policy in late 1919, 34–37; Millerand successfully subverts Feisal-Clemenceau January 6, 1920, agreement, 37–41; gains British support, 39, 40; meaning of the Syrian mandate for France, 42

Ganem, Chekri: and Central Syrian Committee, 27–28

Georges-Picot, François, 13 n, 22, 30–31; negotiates Anglo-French agreement of 1916, 10–12; meets Hussein in 1917, 17–18; warns Ribot about Arabia, 19; initial response to Feisal, 19–20; urges Clemenceau to send troops to Middle East, 20; curbed by Allenby, 21; questions French policy towards Feisal on eve of Paris Peace Conference, 23; and Zionism, 25; meets Feisal at Peace Conference, 29

Gouraud, Henri, 39; opposes Clemenceau's conciliatory policy towards Feisal, 34–35; warns of growing Arab nationalism in Syria, 36–37; believes French position in Middle East is precarious, 38; prepares for decisive action against Feisal, 40; sends ultimatums to Feisal, 41; extols benefits of a French mandate, 42

Goût, Jean, 10, 34, 35

Grey, Edward, 10; rejects British suggestions to oust France from Syria, 7; initiates discussions leading to Sykes-Picot agreement, 9; claims that Sykes-Picot agreement and British pledges to Hussein were not incompatible, 14, 33; Syria is reserved for France, 20

Hardinge, Charles: recognizes France as dominant power in Syria, 39

Hogarth, David, 14

Hussein, Sherif of Mecca, 10, 11, 14, 16, 21, 23, 33; and correspondence with McMahon, 8–9; and the Arab Revolt, 15; and Ribot's plans for the postwar Middle East, 16–19; meets Picot, 17–18

Ibn Saud, 16

Italy: threat to prewar France's position in Middle East, 5; response to the Sykes-Picot agreement, 14–15

Kemal, Mustapha, 38, 40

Kitchener, Horatio: and plans to remove France from Syria, 7; wants discussions with France to clarify Middle Eastern position, 8

Lawrence, T. E., 17, 19; as Feisal's adviser at Paris Peace Conference, 28–29, 30

Leygues, Georges, 10; and France's prewar position in the Middle East, 5; concerned about England's anti-French policies, 32–33

Lloyd George, David, 15, 20, 21, 30, 35, 38; meets Clemenceau in London, 1918, 23; interprets Sykes-Picot agreement and McMahon's October 24, 1915, letter to mean that independent Syria must be created, 28, 32, 33; conflict with Clemenceau at Paris Peace Conference, 28, 31–32; seeks compromise with France, 33–34; appreciates the significance of Clemenceau's resignation in 1920, 37

Macdonogh, G. M.: Arab independence means British control, 22

McMahon, Henry, 15, 23, 28, 33; anti-French sentiments, 7, 9; the October 24, 1915, letter to Hussein protects future French claims to Syria, Palestine, and Lebanon, 8–9; maintains that Sykes-Picot agreement does not contradict British agreement with Arabs, 14

49

Margerie, Bruno de, 10
Maxwell, John, 7
Maysalun, 41
Millerand, Alexandre, 10, 43; hostile to January 6, 1920, agreement, 37–39; and the reintroduction of "autonomies," 37, 39; disagreement with Great Britain concerning response to Feisal and Syrian independence, 38–39; prepares to depose Feisal, 39–40; and ultimatum to Feisal, 41; and the role of France in Syria, 40, 42; impatient with Gouraud's caution regarding Feisal, 41
Milner, Alfred: and compromise proposal for France and Feisal, 30
Murray, Archibald, 20

Nicholas II: agrees to France's 1915 plans except on question of Palestine, 5–6
Nicolson, Arthur: negotiates with Picot, 10–11
Nivelle, Robert, 17

Paléologue, Maurice, 10: and France's Middle Eastern policy in 1915, 5–6
Pichon, Stéphen, 10, 21, 33; initial response to Feisal, 19–20; believes Feisal will need France, 20; Sykes-Picot agreement the foundation of France's Middle Eastern policies, 23, 26, 28; French policy towards Feisal on eve of Paris Peace Conference, 24; French response to threat of Arab nationalism, 24; and the meaning of the Anglo-French declaration of November 7, 1918, 24; changes French policy towards Zionists, 24–26; and Balfour Declaration, 25–26; and French Middle Eastern policy on the eve of peace conference, 26; accepts the mandate concept, 26–27; and negotiations with Feisal, 28; surprised by Feisal's rejections, 30; despite failure French policy hinges on Sykes-Picot agreement, 30–31; policies supported by French public opinion, 32
Picot. *See* Georges-Picot, François
Poincaré, Raymond: and threats to France's prewar position in the Middle East, 5
Provisional Agreement of January 6, 1920, 44–45; reasons for, 35–36, 43; enemies of, 36–37, 39

Ribot, Alexandre, 10, 15; formulates France's Middle Eastern policies in 1917, 16–17; foresees conflict with Arabs, 18; and conflict with England concerning Arabia, 19; and Zionists, 25
Russia: and France's wartime Middle Eastern policies, 5–6, 13, 14

St. Jean de Maurienne, Conference of, 15, 23
San Remo Conference, 38; significance of, 39
Slousch, Naoum, 24
Sokolow, Nahum, 25, 26
Sonnino, Sidney: and response to Sykes-Picot agreement, 14–15
Storrs, Ronald: wants England to control Syria, 7
Sykes, Mark, 20, 21, 22; and mid-1915 British plans for postwar Middle East, 7–8; negotiates Anglo-French agreement with Picot, 11–13; meets Picot and Hussein in 1917, 17–18
Sykes-Picot agreement (Anglo-French Agreement of 1916), 17, 18, 19, 29, 30, 34, 39, 43–44; discussions leading to, 9–13; map of, 13; Russia agrees to it, 13; no contradiction with McMahon's promise to Hussein, 14, 33; gains Italy's support, 14–15; the key to France's wartime Middle Eastern policies, 14, 16, 26, 28, 34; Grey recognizes that agreement reserved Syria for France, 14, 20, 33; is rejected by England, 21, 22, 23; is interpreted by Lloyd George to mean that Syria should be independent, 28, 32, 33
Syrian National Congress, 37–38

Tardieu, André, 32; and Zionism, 25–26
Temps, Le, 32

Viviani, René, 10: reaffirms France's interest in Middle East, 8

Wilson, Woodrow, 22, 24, 25, 26, 27, 31, 37, 42; suggests inquiry commission at Peace Conference, 28
Wingate, Reginald: anti-French sentiments, 7

Young Turks, 15

Zionism: and France, 24–26